RELEASE MOMENTS

Forgiveness Learned, Strength to Overcome & Empowered to Live

ROSETTA PRIESTLY

Enhanced DNA
DEVELOP. NURTURE. ACHIEVE.
Publishing Division

DenolaBurton@EnhancedDNA1.com
www.EnhancedDNAPublishing.com
317-537-1438

RELEASE MOMENTS: Forgiveness Learned, Strength to Overcome and Empowered to Live

Cover created by Byron Scott Elliott, Jr. - Blacksheep Collective
Editing by Michelle P. Jones, LLC

ISBN-13: 978-1-7369079-6-2
Library of Congress Number: 2021918148

ACKNOWLEDGEMENTS

To those supporters who have gone on to glory, the Heavy Hitters in the faith, and my prayer warriors, Mrs. Gertrude Willis, Leon W. Marshall, Laura and Donald Cosby, Mr. Michael Nickleson, Kendall L. Priestly, and Mrs. Nancy J. Willis; thank you! The prayers of the righteous availeth much, and I am proof of that!

To my supporters who are taking this journey and faith-walk with me through the good, the bad and the ugly, thank you! My personal Spiritual Heavy Hitters, Mrs. Rosetta Marshall, Uncle Frank Willis, Cindy Robinette, Pastor Charles Willis, Pastor Samuel Willis, and Lady Charlesetta Willis.

To my children, Elizabeth, April, Kendra, Antonio, Son-in-loves B.J., Greg, and all my beautiful grandchildren, thank you for your continuous support, love, and prayers.

Mere words cannot express my eternal gratitude for you all being the greatest blessings in my life. Thank you from the deep crevasses of my heart! For sure, without GOD, I would not be here, but also, without all of you touching my life, I could not have gotten here either. You are more precious to me than I can fully express, and more valuable than money or gems can buy. You are priceless to me.

Rosetta Priestly

TABLE OF CONTENTS

Rosetta Priestly

LETTER TO READERS

While growing in my faith, I learned a lot about spiritual warfare. Once I heard Apostle John Eckhardt say, *"Rejection prevents someone from giving or receiving love from God or other people. This spirit of rejection opens the door for other spirits to enter a person's life, including anxiety, hurt, unforgiveness, and bitterness. It joins up with rebellion, causing double mindedness in individuals. Almost everyone has experienced rejection in life."*

People can be rejected for many reasons, like gender, skin color, economic status, size, and/or shape, while never realizing they are dealing with a spirit. The spirit of rejection is a significant stronghold in many people's lives, but it does not have to be. We can choose to accept God's love and be set free from the spirit of rejection and all its bondage or not. I challenge you to consider that by not making a decision, you have unconsciously made the decision to allow forces outside you, and that are contrary to God's purpose for your life to make decisions on your behalf. I am here today because I needed deliverance from the stronghold of rejection, and I decided to find deliverance, acceptance and love in Jesus Christ, my Lord and Savior.

There are many published books that go in depth on the topic of rejection and the freedom from its demonic stronghold. A remarkable tool I used, and I suggest reading, is John Eckhardt's *"Deliverance and Spiritual Warfare Manual."* It will give you great insight and understanding of deliverance's practical application in a person's life. I just wanted to give an overview, because I am giving my testimony of how God delivered me from the stronghold of rejection. Every person's situation and experiences are different. What I used may not work for you, but the Holy Bible is the universal tool for all life's issues and/or situations.

I thank God for all the false starts I experienced with this book. I am more grateful for the revelation from this point on, which allows me to finish this in excellence for His glory! Holy Spirit empower me to do this!!! I birthed this book from my Spirit when I realized I was existing, rather than living out the God-ordained purpose for my life. All I know for sure is the journey has been incredible, challenging, confusing and emotionally grueling. Despite it all, I still have praise in my mouth to glorify God for it all! My life may not be ideal from some people's perspective, but it is the ordained and purposed life God has given me. It is genuine and authentic. May each reader gain inspiration from the seeds of do not quit, believe in God Almighty, and fight for what you love found within the pages of this book. Even if you love you, fight to be the absolute best person God desires you to be!

My heart's desire for this book is to inspire, empower and encourage every person who reads it. God has shown me how to reach a nation simply by being open and honest in the telling of my story. What God said to me was both pivotal and powerful due to the spiritual battle that has ensued as I birthed this book. I know what I have gone through in the earth realm, and if that is any indication, the battle in the spirit realm has been of a magnitude that was thoroughly destructive to the devil's agenda and kingdom. When the concept for this book was first downloaded into me, I did not think I could inspire anyone with my life's release moments, but God knew better. My prayer is that you, the reader, will be encouraged, enriched, and uplifted by this creative work. Ephesians 1:3-6 states, "*Blessed be the God and father of our Lord Jesus Christ, who has blessed us with every spiritual blessing in the heavenly places in Christ, just as He chose us in Him before the foundation of the world. That we should be holy and without blame before Him in love, having predestined us to adopt as sons by Jesus Christ to Himself, according to the good pleasure of His will, the praise and glory of His grace, by which He made us accepted in the beloved.*" I had to learn for myself, my freedom is in Jesus, and that life issues do not go away when I do not face them, but when I chose to overcome them. There is a level of freedom that inspires me to tell others how it is possible, especially as I continue to learn how to live life victoriously.

The Lord revealed to me that the seeds of rejection planted in my heart occurred during my childhood from family members and others who had direct influence over my upbringing, and who guided or helped build the foundation of my faith in Christ that I stand on today. In June 2018, I went on a fast and sought God to reveal the spiritual reasons why the onslaught of negativity, lies, doubts, fears, and/or worries were showing up unexpectedly in my life, and why I kept repeating destructive cycles. Consequently, the Lord showed me how to get to the root of these spiritual issues and receive the deliverance my soul ached for.

God revealed to me that the issues going on in my life were rooted in my fear of man, fear of rejection, fear of not having enough resources, fear of not being enough, and the fear of failure simmering just beneath the surface of my spirit man. What I had not realized is that at different times during my spiritual journey, I have had destructive words spoken to me.

Negative and hurtful words that I interpreted and internalized as rejection by the people who had access to me. Those words had planted the seeds of rejection in my heart and mind and were the words God used to show me I needed healing and deliverance from the spirit of rejection. Until God revealed it to me, I did not know it was controlling me. Remembering those words brought back memories as far back as those I experienced as a five-year-old. Not from what was said, but from who said it triggered the memories, which forced me to become that five-year-old girl who had not grown up.

Even though I had been freed and delivered from many fears and other forms of rejection. I had not dealt with the rejection of the two most important people in my life, my mother, and my former pastor. I often asked myself, *"Why did I have an overwhelming desire to talk to them, but a debilitating fear of confronting those two individuals?"* I did not realize how crippling this was until that fateful day in June 2018. That realization led me to repent for carrying those ungodly fears around in my heart and mind, while they grew stronger day by day and were the basis of the behaviors and emotions, I experienced that did not make sense to me. God promised He would heal my heart and deliver me from the spirit of rejection once I surrendered control of my life to Him. As I continue my journey to deliverance, God has given me a greater understanding of His acceptance, which overrules every rejection, whether real or imagined, that has ever occurred or will occur in my life.

FOREWORD

by
Namun and Rhasheeda Hague

A metamorphosis is the process by which an entity completely changes forms to become something completely different. Most commonly, this change is associated with caterpillars becoming butterflies.

This change is also symbolic of the change God desires to show in each of us. That we are so dynamic that we resemble an entirely new being. The changes show the culmination of years of learning and growing at the feet of Jesus. We no longer look, act, or even reflect the person we previously were.

Potential remains unrealized opportunities until a person becomes fortified with enough supernatural strength that transcends who they are. They have become a new creation. The old identification is passed away and all things have become new. Now, even problems and situations take on a new perspective. Nothing is realized from the previous point of view. What previously may have been impossible now falls under a different category, achievable.

"*Release Moments*" ventures into one such story. Read along and learn the significant effects that a life of prayer can have. This impact is not only moving the one praying but also touches those around them. The weight associated with carrying your own burdens, the pain of feeling like you are walking alone, and/or the frustration you feel when you are not progressing as desired, are all feelings that are impossible to overcome on your own. Through prayer and the guidance of the Holy Spirit, you will overcome them!

Light and life go hand in hand. The life you are now living opens you up to a new realm of possibilities. The darkness that once surrounded you have been shattered by the brightness of how you are currently living. Hope helps you build a better life for yourself. This allows more and more light to shine in and through you. This radiance will begin drawing others, causing them to wonder, how did you make it?

Typically, this growth is not something one must volunteer for. It comes from personal hardships. When situations mount like a tidal wave, people feel as if they are drowning from all the pressure. That becomes the spark that causes them to seek the Lord like never before. Life has come to a place where the bearer must remove the things hindering them and seek a change. For without it, the place of hope becomes lost. The storms of life rage wildly, challenging focus and faith.

This status of deferred hope leaves people feeling sick and dejected. For without hope as an anchor, a person loses their footing and lose their focus. The ability to persevere despite adverse conditions results in staying close to Christ. And the closer we remain to Christ, the more difficult it becomes to experience the onset of death, destruction, and despair.

A prayer warrior is an individual whose faith leads them to pray, believing that their prayers are enough to overcome the present course of any situation. The prayer warrior refuses to take no for an answer. He/She has developed the spiritual fortitude to understand that an actual change to the eventual outcome depends on their ability to reach God through prayer. They are not merely going through the motions; they are skillfully and purposely getting before the Lord to send, create and/or generate enough activity that things change.

Prayer warriors realize their potential in any situation. They truly believe that getting before the Lord proves nothing is impossible for Him. Their faith through prayer will ensure they will not have to experience the same problems, limits, and/or barriers that those who do not pray may experience. Hardships may have started the issue or situation, but the power of prayer unleashes the opportunities of Heaven. Gather your strength and begin believing that life's toughest situations will not stop you.

Notice how this journey of faith took one woman from a place of despair to happiness and contentment. Rosetta never believed that life could be like this. Watch as the metamorphosis transforms her entire world. Before your very eyes, she officially transitions from hopeless to a faith filled individual.

And the joy that now fills her heart is helping her live her best life now. It was not instant! It was not overnight, but it was fulfilling. Everything surrounding her is subject to change based on the work that is going on within her.

"*Release Moments*" is also a celebration of life. Where those who have overcome or those who are overcoming can rejoice after sharing in this testimony. The gems of inspiration found within these pages reflect and sparkle with radiance due to the wondrous works of the Lord. Remember, He is no respecter of person. What He has done for one, He will do for all. So be of good cheer, your heavenly father knows exactly what you have need of and truly desires to give it to you. He is our benefactor. He loads us up daily with his blessings and benefits.

Allow "*Release Moments*" to encourage you to carve out a new legacy in life. Let it infuse hope within you and a desire to live a life you always believed was beyond your reach. Give the new you a chance to thrive and be fulfilled. You will be filled with His power, His presence, and His goodness. Living on your own and for yourself is complicated, but living for Christ endows you with love, life, and liberty.

Namun and Rhasheeda Hague
Wisdom for the Wilderness Ministry
Business: *Namun Rhasheeda Godly Grounded Enterprise LLC (NRGG Enterprise)*

INTRODUCTION

My story begins with how God delivered me from the stronghold of rejection. The rejection that found its way into almost every aspect of my life. I cannot say when it began, what I can say is I believe it began with my mother, her authoritative ways, and my inability to emotionally bond with her throughout my childhood. However, that is not where it ended. My feelings of rejection showed up in my relationship with my stepfather, as it related to how I felt about the absence of my biological father from my life. Those two are not the only experiences I have had with rejection. They speak to the beginning of my relationship with the spirit of rejection and how it took up residence in my life.

Rejection prevents someone from giving or receiving love from God and/or other people and acts as the doorkeeper who opens the door for other spirits to enter the person, including fear, hurt, unforgiveness, and/or bitterness. Rejection does not act alone; it links with rebellion and causes the individual to experience double mindedness. People are rejected for many reasons, like their gender, skin color, economic status, size, shape, etc. Almost everyone has experienced rejection at some point in their life. The spirit of rejection can be a major stronghold in the lives of many people, but he does not have to be. As free moral agents, we can accept Jesus' love and be loosed from the spirit of rejection and its all-encompassing bondage.

Release allows or enables someone to escape from confinement and/or to be set free. A moment is a momentary period in time.

I pray this book inspires everyone who reads it to know that there is freedom, hope, love, joy, and peace through Christ Jesus available to them. It is only after they have faced the perplexing issues in their lives that they will know how to traverse the journey they find themselves on. It gives them a tremendous capacity to read and understand the living testimony of how God delivered me from the spirit of rejection. And as a believer, a daughter, a sister, mother, wife, divorcee, grandmother, minister of the Gospel, Biblical counselor, entrepreneur, and encourager for God, I pray you are inspired to live fully as a yielded vessel for God's glory. I was assigned this project to share how God turned tragedies into triumphs and strengthened me to tell this story with authority and power. Ephesians 1:3-6 states, *"Blessed be the God and father of our Lord Jesus Christ, who has blessed us with every spiritual blessing in the heavenly places in Christ, just as He chose us in Him before the foundation of the world, that we should be holy and without blame before Him in love, having predestined us to be adopted as sons by Jesus Christ to Himself, according to the good pleasure of His will, to the praise and glory of His grace, by which He made us accepted in the beloved."*

Let us dive into Acceptance! Acceptance is a rendering of the Hebrew reason, *"delight,"* as found in Isaiah 60:7. It identifies God's delight in His redeemed people in the Messianic era, when their gifts are joyful and in profuse abundance, and *"...shall come up with acceptance, on mine altar."* In this regard, acceptance is the redeeming grace and the basis of divine favor. It is the *"living, holy sacrifice"* acceptable to God, as written in Romans 12:1 (compare Titus 3:4-6).

Regarding my story, Romans 3:24 KJV refers to one being freely justified by His (God's) grace through the redemptive powers in Christ Jesus. As I became more aware of the need for acceptance in my own life, the following statement became a foundational truth in my life: "*I am convinced I will have more faith in what God speaks to me than what the devil is speaking to deceive me.*"

Acceptance is the state of being acceptable and accepted: the action of consenting to receive or undertake something offered; or the action or process of being received as adequate or suitable, typically to be admitted into a group.

The previously referenced definitions for acceptance are a necessary pause in the action that brings clarity to the journey of rejection to acceptance I have experienced, and the reason I have chosen to focus solely on the acceptance of God.

It is only through acceptance that one can embrace a certain state in life and come to the presence of mind that promises there is something different, greater, and/or more blessed than they could have ever imagined being prepared for them. By accepting this fundamental truth, you give yourself permission to change the perception and perspective of who you are and the purpose for your birth. I am not telling you what someone told me. I am sharing with you the fundamental truths from the lessons on acceptance I have learned that have changed my life. God's acceptance of me and the excitement I have at sharing this message in this book have brought it all full circle for me and is forever imprinted both upon my life and the pages of this book.

I have noticed God has always been part of my life and showed Himself to me in many ways, even when I did not recognize them. I could not appreciate it then, as I can now that God has maintained and sustained me beyond all the chaos or adversities I have experienced in my lifetime. As they say, hindsight is 20/20. I am certain that if I did not have the foundation in God that I stand on daily, I would not be here today. I am so grateful for every Sunday school teacher, VBS teacher, minister, prophetess, encourager, hugger, and/or every other person who shared the message of Jesus Christ and Him crucified with me that has blessed me tremendously! After accepting Jesus as my Savior, I did not know that my life was going to be as intense as a bending and winding road on a dark and stormy night. I have experienced more issues and devastations that are meant to steal my joy, kill me physically and destroy me spiritually early in life. Like the first-born son of King David and Bathsheba, *"I was shaped in iniquity; and in sin did my mother conceive me..."* (Psalms 51:5) and speaks to my beginning and the fact that my parents were not married when I was born.

It is God's sovereign wisdom that orchestrates my life, and who dictates a warrior is not made overnight. Their training begins early in life to ensure they have ample time to develop the skills and techniques needed while learning the strategies that win battles. As I continue to learn, I must fight the good fight of faith and live a lifestyle of Christianity before the world. When I look back, I could have died in my mother's birth canal, but God made a way for me to get here through a C-section. I like to think of it as Christ's mighty hand of divinity moved to ensure a powerful representative for Him would be born into the world. Only God could do it! I was born into the stigma of a child born out of wedlock. However, in today's society, it is a commonality, and no longer has the stigma and/or reprimand in the social networks of the Church and/or society.

The young women in my family learned how to work hard, take care of our responsibilities, and establish a family unit to care for and share in each other's lives, loves, hurts, shames, accomplishments, pain, upsets and/or life defining moments. This was most evident in my mother's and grandmother's relationship, and in how my mother cared for my grandmother. Later in life, I learned my mother prayed for many years and asked the Lord to birth only two children: a girl and a boy. God answered her prayer, but it did not happen in the socially accepted way with the security of a husband and part of the nuclear family. My mother accepted me as an answer to her prayer. An answer that did not feel like a blessing that is normally seen or felt, to me. She learned how to manage a budget, take care of her responsibilities, and raise me with the limited education she had to fight for.

My mother was determined and had great fervor to work hard and do what was necessary to survive as a single parent against all odds in the 1970s. Seven years later, when my brother was born, she still persevered and survived. This brief interjection of my mother's story here shows that I did not come from an ideal nor privileged background, but from hard work and doing the best with what you had available to you. As a matter of fact, it highlights the struggle I experienced to be born and the struggles of acceptance that introduced me to and gave me the keys to building a relationship with the spirit of rejection that I have struggled with throughout my life. Although I have seen and experienced more than most, I can now recognize how God has always been in control of every facet of my life while navigating my path to get me to this point. I tell you, my God is an awesome God, and I am grateful He saw past my circumstances and saw me!

So, the acceptance of responsibility was instilled within me. I learned the importance of hard work as it was modeled before me. It shaped my definition and expectations of what hard work looked like. What I know today that I did not know back then is that it is not the only perspective, but the one passed down from generation to generation. Those were not the only examples shown to me, they were the ones I accepted as the norm, while discounting the validity and accessibility of the others because they were unfamiliar and out of my norm. The other examples and/or methods I discounted were being an entrepreneur and/or having creative and witty ideas, because they were not an option for me, my mother, nor my grandmother's generation. Which is why I did not entertain those thoughts. Nothing in my life gave me permission to consider them an option, example, and/or method when working hard. I only knew the struggle of a single mother who worked hard to raise her children and be a responsible, although limited, and productive member of society. I was taught to work hard with my hands, be diligent in doing so, and everything will be well in life. Talent was not needed nor necessary. I was instructed to be committed to the life before me and/or that I was born into. However, God showed me a different way. God showed me the world beyond the environment I was raised in and continues to show me how to live an abundant and limitless life today.

During my early development, I internalized and personalized this training as a negative aspect of my relationship with my mother. I interpreted it as being rejected and not being embraced by her, which led me to not accept myself, not learn how to love myself, not being able to comprehend the value I offered my family and the world, and/or why I felt I could not emotionally relate or connect with her.

I was taught to follow instructions, and when I obeyed, I would be rewarded. The opposite was true, when I did not obey, I got punished. These lessons were learned early in my life. Unlike today, there were no timeouts and/or counting to ten. Discipline was applied when you did not do what you were told. Simply put, you either did what you were told, or you would suffer the consequences. This became a mantra I lived by, and that showed up in my relationship with God. I believed this was the ideal way to grow closer to Him. By obeying His instructions, I would be rewarded, and by not obeying, I would suffer the consequences. This in no way was the total truth about God. However, as I reflected on this, God began to reiterate how He created humanity after He made the provisions, they would need to sustain them. A realization dawned on me that helped me determine my relationship with my mother and others in my life differently. I knew my mother loved me by her actions, even if it was rarely said to my brother and I while we were growing up. Today, I know she did the best she could with what she had available to her, and that she rarely said 'I love you' to us because it was rarely said to her. The lessons I learned early structured my life going forward. What I once beheld as structured, I now understand, is rigid without the ability to accept anything outside of what I considered normal.

My acceptance was part of God's plan from the beginning. However, the enemy of my soul, the liar himself, the devil, worked in my life creating blockages, rejections, negativity, and disdain, since he discovered my purpose is a threat to the furtherance of the kingdom of darkness as it relates to his vision and mission here on the earth. He knew that if I ever came into the fullness of who I am in Christ, I would be one of his greatest adversaries.

I pose this question to you, the reader: "*Have you believed the lies of the devil or believed your thoughts more than believing the unfailing and proven truth of a Holy, loving, and righteous God?*" When I could grasp this question for what it was and its purpose for appearing in my mind and heart, I was strengthened, empowered, and encouraged to finish this book. It taught me the importance of being transparent about genuinely accepting the truth that I am accepted by the Beloved! What I have learned is when attempting to answer that question, it leads to more demoralizing and destructive questions like "*Do I even believe I need the approval of man over God? Do I believe I am not good enough, smart enough, loved enough, etc.*" built on a foundation of lies and deceit designed to distract and detour the destiny God has planned for me! If you are willing to consider the source and reason for the question appearing in your life and give yourself permission to bask in the love and acceptance available to you and designed for you to experience daily from God, you will feel the same way!

Maybe it is me, but when I get a revelation from God's word and apply it to my life, I am taking heed of what God is truly doing in my life! Resulting in me being blessed by the Lord! I love the fact that God loves me so much. He blessed me with the mother I have! I recognize this now, even though I did not value her and the role she played in my life during my childhood, as I do now. That is because God enlarged my ability to accept her and others for who they are! I am grateful and thankful I still have my mother and her wisdom that I pull from daily as I help make her golden years joyful and full of love. My mother and grandmother have been major influences who have helped shape me into who I am today. However, what is upsetting and/or disturbing is I had to mature and grow before I could know God and experience His mercy, grace, love, wisdom, understanding, and joy, as well as correction that directly results from my obedience to God. All of which has led me to appreciate, accept, and love them both as gifts from God.

The acceptance I speak of is a lifelong journey and ongoing process that allows me to trust, submit, rely on, and completely obey God as He blesses me daily with new mercies. I have experienced enough of the lies of the enemy of my soul that I can emphatically say, *"enough is enough!"*

I do not want to act like everybody is brought up in a Christian, faith-based, Jesus Christ-centered, Bible believing home, because I know that is not true. However, to know about Jesus and truly have a relationship with Him is available to any and everyone. The problem that many unbelievers face, and some believers, is that they often buy into the lies, schemes, and utter deception of the devil, hoping they will fill the void with something other than having God in their life. This is a void that only God can fill. Most people allow rejection, especially from family and those closest to them, to scar them so greatly they become people pleasers instead of living a life hid in Jesus, and that pleases God. I am not judging anyone, because if I did, I would also condemn myself. At a point in my life, I went through the same thing, which is why I can speak about it.

There is nothing this world wants more than an audience to celebrate SIN, and all the horrendous life-altering effects it has on a person's body, mind, and spirit until it completely kills their desire to live, steals their joy and/or destroys their relationships with others, because they cannot see past what they need and/or want.

One of my favorite childhood songs is *"Jesus Loves Me"*. Now when I first learned that song, I did not understand or have the revelation that I have now. Every time I hear or sing it, I am reminded of what that truly means, Jesus loves me! Although it may appear so simple to some people, it is not. Truly knowing and applying those lyrics to my life has been life affirming and changing. *"Jesus loves me, this I know for the Bible tells me so!"* How can I understand acceptance if I do not understand the love of God towards me? Jesus loves Me! When I sang this song as a little girl while being trained in the truth, it spoke to my innocence. I did not have the experience to truly know that fact for myself. As I grew in life and in the knowledge of Jesus Christ, that song and so many others have grounded me and helped me build a strong foundation in the assurance and knowledge that Jesus loves me. Even when I did not love Him, He still loved me. Now that is powerful!

Being a flawed human, my expectations, desires and/or imagination were based on what I saw and/or experienced with the interpersonal relationships in my home, the television shows I watched, and my worldly interactions. I lacked the knowledge to know why I would even want a love like the one offered by God. I learned that whatever your fantasy may be, can quickly become your reality if you make it your god. It will cause you to experience a magnitude of disappointment, despair, and rejection that becomes deeply rooted in your life. What happened in my life taught me that I needed to change dance partners from dancing with the world to dancing with God to benefit from the love and acceptance I lacked in my life. I accepted the thought intellectually that God loved me, but not spiritually. I was taught in Sunday school, Vacation Bible school, Bible study, and Sunday services about this awesome God. However, early in my life, I always asked what else is there to God beyond these moments in the Church. I desired, let me change that, I needed more. I needed to know how to live my life when I am not in the Church, and experience God's love in my everyday life.

As a young girl, I knew there was more to God, but did not learn about the many aspects of His character, how to trust Him, and how to apply His word to my life and/or live a Christian lifestyle. Discipling has its place in the organized Church, but as the scriptures say, I must seek God for myself. In Hebrews 11:6, we are instructed to believe that God is who He proclaims Himself to be, and that we must seek Him. It assures the believer, "...*that He is a rewarder of them that diligently seek Him.*" When I sought God out, asked Him questions, and learned to yearn for His presence, my relationship with God deepened. It took me to a place in our relationship I had never experienced before, and that I now dwell in daily now. Just as the scripture says, "*But without faith, it is impossible to please Him; for he that cometh to God must believe He is...*" When I understood who Jesus is, it was easy for me to receive the love and acceptance He offers those who have faith in Him. The building of our relationship did not stop there. I had to believe Jesus forgave me of my sins when he completed his perfect work at Calvary. I also had to learn to be obedient to His word, move and/or act when prompted by the Holy Spirit, which taught me how to love Him more. The gospel, the good news, has ministered to me throughout my childhood. When I was eleven years old, I accepted with the understanding of a child the love Jesus has for me. It did not occur to my eleven-year-old self that the bliss from the newness, and the excitement and joy of being a newborn Christian, would be attacked and almost snuffed out from the trauma that happened to me a few months later. Like so many other Christians, I realize that what I experienced did not mean God did not love me.

Down through the years, the confessions I made to God were and will continue to be challenged to see if my faith and/or my confession are true. I have heard many ask, and if I am being honest, I have asked *"why me?"* *"Why did I have to endure those life challenges?"* Each time I asked, I received the same answer, *"Why not you?"* *"Why do you question why you had to go through that?"* My life dramatically changed during my formative years between the ages of seven and fifteen. I faithfully went to the Church while being taught about God and His word, but not understanding its significance in my life. Then when all the major changes happened: the birth of a younger brother, a new stepfather, the home raid that brought me face to face with a fear I had never experienced and led to me being fearful of almost everything, and me becoming self-absorbed while blaming myself for everything that went wrong in my home and becoming a teenage unwed mother. The despair and mental pain I felt became the food I received nourishment from both day and night, as my tears watered my sense of hopelessness. A sense of hopelessness, the enemy of my soul fertilized as he planted suicidal thoughts while trying to convince me that suicide offered the relief I sought and was the answer to the questions rolling around in my heart and mind.

When I accepted Jesus as my Lord and Savior, I did not know about the spiritual, physical, and mental attacks that would be unleashed from making that choice.

According to 2 Timothy 3:5-7, they will have a form of godliness, but will deny the power of the word of God and will lack the life-guiding knowledge that only comes from the indwelling presence of the Holy Spirit. They were attracted to having a mental knowledge of Jesus, His love and all His wonderful works, but not the spiritual realization that made them want to love, obey, and be conformed to the image of Jesus. However, the benefit afforded to believers is that whoever accepts Jesus as their personal Savior and obeys the word of GOD will be accepted by God. I came to the place where the rubber met the road, and I had to accept Jesus Christ. In every person's life, there will come a time when everyone must make the choice for themselves. The same choice I made. There was nothing exciting about the experiences I had as a child, however, they were necessary and critical to my Spiritual growth and development.

Pastor Johnson said during one of her sermons that *"once you have been delivered from what man thinks about you; and you stop going to man-check clinics to get diagnoses from perfectly imperfect people, just like you, you have finally learned whose opinion truly matters."* It forced me to refocus on the One who I must give an account to. It makes obeying and pleasing GOD the priority!

Rosetta Priestly

CHAPTER 1: Rough Beginnings with Lasting Meanings

The egg stage of a butterfly is relative to the egg stage of a human being. When I look at a butterfly, I see the beauty of God in its color, flight, and existence. Now, if I could regard an insect as one of God's creations with that type of reverence, why couldn't I identify that same beauty and uniqueness within myself? I am a created being formed and put together in my mother's womb by the mighty hand of God. God ordained the egg that became Rosetta from the two vessels who contributed the two sets of twenty-three chromosomes. In the same way that everything I experienced in my life is necessary to who I am today, the unlikely matching of my mother and father was necessary to ensure I was created as designed by God.

I will compare the transformational stages of a butterfly to my life, as I have grown, failed, overcome, and am empowered to be here today. I pray you will accept and understand this is my journey, but since I am not alone on this earth, there may be times when you identify yourself in my story. If you do, it is my prayer that you gain clarity, strength, and comfort as you begin your journey. I have traversed many life situations, but I cannot write and give the details of each of them. What I can do is obey God and talk about the areas that were the most traumatic. My transformation has resulted from God's Holy Spirit, which empowered me to live when the natural thing would be to die before I could tap into my potential. Let *"Release Moments"* bring clarity on how God taught me to forgive and strengthened me with His Word to overcome situations. The only way this happened was by the power of God, through the guidance of His Holy Spirit. What I did not know as a child growing up was that God had His hand on my life, and I did not understand it, but now I appreciate it even more.

Ages (0-7): From my viewpoint, there were spiritual seeds put in me, but there were also dysfunctional, fearful, confusing, and academic seeds put in me. All concurrently with the regular living of life. I thank God, that He was my covering, but I still had to live each day. My egg stage had developmental issues far beyond my control but contributed to the dysfunction I normalized during my early years. Clearly, the way I began was not the way I ended.

There is nothing more devastating to a child than being rejected by the person or persons who are supposed to love them. The devastation I felt was from the disconnect between me and my parents, and I was unaware of why the disconnect has occurred. The disconnect left me scratching my head, trying to figure out what was so terrible that it deserved automatic rejection. No one offered an explanation. The people I expected to offer an explanation were acting like the rejection did not require an explanation. Therefore, it became a destructive force in my life when it compounded the existing problems in my life even more.

My earliest memory of being rejected in this manner happened at age five, when I visited with my biological father for the last time during my childhood. In my five-year-old mind and heart, I believed whatever I did was so severe it caused him to leave without so much as a goodbye. For the next two years, I remember only knowing father figures, like my uncles, who are part of my extended family, and influenced my young life.

When I turned seven, my brother was born, and my mother married my stepfather, who became the new father figure in my life. Nightly, the same questions plagued my thoughts, "*Where was my father? Why did he not want me anymore? Why did my grandmother and aunts remind me often that my stepfather was not my father?*" How was I supposed to deal with a total stranger who was forced into my life, when I had not processed, understood, or accepted my father was not present in my life? I was unwilling to accept this forced change in my family. A new brother and a new stepdad! This new familial dynamic had a rough start from not having contact with my father while thinking, "*what did I do that was so bad he did not want to see me anymore?*"

After having my mother all to myself for seven years, I felt like I began to compete for her attention with my baby brother. I was not ready for any of this. For all intents and purposes, I was the live-in sitter as my stepfather supervised. My role in the family instantly changed. I had to oversee the household while my mother worked. For a seven-year-old, I had many life changes that occurred simultaneously. I was raised in a household where children were to be seen but not heard. It was an authoritative disciplinarian's house, which taught me valuable lessons throughout my childhood. One of the most important lessons I learned was to obey my parents or suffer the consequences of not doing so. Even as I attempted to make sense of my new reality, I could not remember being told why my father left or stopped visiting me. This memory became a seed that took root as spiritual dis-ease that spread throughout my life. I could not fully grasp the events. Therefore, rejection and abandonment became my constant companions. What I know now, but had no clue of then, is that anything left untreated in your life starts small and then grows like weeds uncontrollably. Over time, it grew into a stronghold in my life, as I am sure it has done in the lives of many others throughout time. Later in life, I learned there is a cure for it, but when I did not use the treatment plan in God's word or acknowledge my need for God's spiritual medication, I unknowingly allowed the infection to spread throughout my mind, heart, and body unchecked. It affected and infected my mind, emotions, and behaviors.

After seven years, I became a big sister and stepchild in the same year, with the two events about six months apart. Talk about a "boom" in life at seven! What choice did I have? I am seven and dependent on my mother for love, security, shelter, and food. Today, in our culture and world, I hope parents and guardians are better at paying attention when children speak about issues that affect and impact their lives. In many instances, it can literally be the difference between life and death! If there had been an adult, I could confide in maybe my perception of my life would have been different.

I can sum the first seven years of my life up to being born to an unwed mother, and barely remembering my biological father. I felt his absence deeply when I witnessed other family members with their fathers. It confused me because I did not understand why. To add insult to injury, after thirteen years of silence, he calls me on the day of my high school graduation. How was I supposed to process that? In my young mind, my first experience with rejection came from my biological father. After which I experienced rejection from my mother when she had my little brother. I did not know how to share her love and attention with anyone, but I learned. With everything I was dealing with, they forced me to accept a stepdad. This was almost too much for a little girl to handle.

The first seven years of my life included experiences that planted the seeds of rejection, fear, and faith in my life. The seeds of faith were planted because my mother made my brother and I go to Church every Sunday with either my grandmother or herself. We were not given a choice in the matter. Being raised in the Church brings both blessings and curses. The challenge is to know the difference. Everything in life has both positives and negatives. God has always been positive, especially when I was young, and the seeds of faith were planted in my life. Now that I am a mother and grandmother, I take my responsibility seriously to share Jesus with my family and teach them that He is the only way we can make it in this world!

My prior experiences showed rejection from key people in my life. At least this is how my child's mind interpreted situations I had no control over. This perception caused me to view life as if I were missing a part of myself and wanting my father to fill the void in my life. He would not or could not fill the void. Leaving me to believe my father abandoned and rejected me because there is something wrong with me. A belief I held on to like a toddler holds on to his/her favorite blanket. I did not have all the information, which left me to make assumptions. As these thoughts plagued my mind, they were being combatted by the Godly principles my maternal grandmother instilled in me. Her prayers and guidance helped me through the rough phases of life and provided me with the adjustments I needed to cope. When

I learned Jesus loves me, it comforted me. Then I knew that someone more significant than my biological father loved me.

What issues have you experienced that have left you wondering why did this happen to me? Who have you talked to about the issue? Do you desire freedom from the issues?

CHAPTER 2: Turbulent Pre-Teen & Teen Years

Ages (8-14): The next stage in a butterfly's life is the larva stage. It's also known as the caterpillar stage. This is the stage where caterpillars only have to eat, and eat, and eat some more. The food eaten by the caterpillar becomes the fuel used later in their various stages of its development (ANSP.org). Caterpillars can grow 100 times their size during this stage. The food I ate during the ages of eight to fourteen consisted of natural physical, spiritual, religious, structure of discipline, and an increased desire to learn academically. The food I consumed fueled my mental, physical, and spiritual growth and development.

At eight years old, a year of living in my new family dynamic, I remember being disciplined for not washing the dishes before going to bed by my mother. My mom began whipping me while I was sleeping. I woke up to my mother hitting me while I experienced excruciating pain with every hit. The next day, while my mom was at work and my stepdad was gone from the house, I put my brother to bed and ran away. I walked two blocks and hid behind a massive tree in the local park for about four hours. After getting everyone worried and out looking for me, I got cold and hungry and went back home. Although everyone, including the authorities, was glad to see me, it was the first time in a long time my mother had shown me that much affection and attention when she hugged and held me tightly.

Although I got the attention I wanted, it was the fear of what would happen afterwards that kept my attention. My mom did not punish me for running away, but I did not know that at the time, and being punished was all I could think about for the rest of the evening. At age nine, I hit puberty and became a young lady with a monthly visitor (that is code for my menstrual cycle). I accepted Jesus Christ as my Savior, at age eleven, and almost died in a police raid (I will explain later). Ages twelve to thirteen, I held on to the anger, fear, hatred from the trauma of the police raid. Age thirteen, first time convicted by God's word to repent of my thoughts and actions and to forgive my stepfather. Then at age fourteen, had first crush, which turned to first boyfriend. After eight months of being boyfriend and girlfriend, I naively lost my virginity. Two months after my fifteenth birthday, I became pregnant with my first child.

Let me unpack this a little for clarity and understanding. I had to be open and honest about what I experienced, but I had to confess and repent of my sins, and I could not blame my parents or my environment for choices I made that affected my life greatly.

At age nine, changes began happening in my body, and I started my menstrual cycle. When this happened, I thought I was dying! My mother thought it was time to tell my family that I had become a young lady. The emotions, cramping, and confusion showed me I was not ready for this part of life. Many other changes occurred that year; we moved multiple times, changed schools, and I faced bullies. Here I am a nine-year-old, trying to understand and accept this new normal in my life.

At age eleven, I was thankful for a pastor who shared the Word of God in a way that inspired my heart to accept Jesus as my Savior. One of the most memorable moments in my life! Almost immediately after that glorious event, one of the most traumatic experiences of my life happened. At eleven years old, I accepted Jesus as my Lord and Savior at a Church revival with two of my cousins. I felt the unction clearly and powerfully, and I know now it was the best decision I ever made. This was a pivotal moment in my life, and before I continue my story, I want to say, just like everyone else, I have a past. As I think about that day, I am reminded that before my dad (stepfather) passed away, he accepted Jesus Christ as his Lord and Savior. Even though I did not ask for or wanted a stepfather early in my life, I learned to love and respect him, and I thank God for him being an integral part of my life. Watching him walk out his Christian journey, before his death, helped me realize everything I went through was necessary. Even if it is only for someone to give his/her life to Jesus after reading or hearing my story, then it has all been worth it.

Also, at age eleven, I experienced one another traumatizing event. My mother worked the night shift, leaving my brother and I home with my stepfather. I did not fully understand the things he did while my mother was at work. The night in question began like every other night, but it did not end that way. From my stepfather's extracurricular activities, the police had been watching him for some time, and that summer night they raided our home. It happened while I was washing dishes. Moments before their intrusion, I had put my brother in the tub for his bath to prepare him to go to bed. Then suddenly, out of nowhere, I heard a loud boom! The police had knocked down the front door of our home.

The police entered our home with their guns drawn. In fear, I ran into my mother's room, only to have an officer find me and point a nine-millimeter gun at my head. He told me, "Don't move or I'll shoot!" He made me lie face down on our floor, and he handcuffed me. They proceeded to get my four-year-old brother out of the bathtub and handcuffed him while he was naked and wet. That event impacted our lives in ways we never could have expected. We both feared the police after the incident. I internalized my fear and became rebellious and depressed. All this happened from my stepfather's activities, and that night he was arrested and later incarcerated. To provide for our family, my mother was forced to work more. There were many financial repercussions that happened to our family after that event. My mother had to pay for an attorney and bear the load of the bills. I was so mad at my stepfather that I wanted to harm him for allowing us to experience such a traumatic event in our young lives. Can you imagine this happening to eleven- and four-year-old children? I later found out that my stepfather was a marijuana dealer. He would make his drug transactions near or in our home.

I write this book as a forty-nine-year-old woman who remembers that day as if it were yesterday! The fears of that day defined who I was for many years. Especially from the devastation and unadulterated fear I experienced when the police handcuffed me. I can honestly say I have been delivered from the emotions and feelings attached to the memory of that event. At some point, I realized that event could have had a different outcome. It could have been the end of my life, but God!!! I am also aware that had these events happened today, they could have had a vastly different and/or tragic outcome. I realize many children have experienced worse things than this and have not survived it. I am grateful Jesus kept us through all those events to be here today to tell the story.

From that point on, I rejected my stepfather's authority and blamed him for this life-threatening event that traumatized both me and my brother. For two years, I bottled up my anger, bitterness, and fear. In my mind, my stepfather was the issue. After serving his time, he was released and entered our home again. I rebelled even more against him because I was still scared, hurt, angry and fearful that the same event could happen again. I would get disciplined for my behavior, but it did not change the fact that I was angry at his presence in our home and, if I am being honest, with his very existence. One day when I was thirteen, the tension in our home was so thick you could cut it with a knife. My stepfather told me to do something, and in response to his command, I blew up in front of my mother and said I hated him. Then I stormed off to my room. My mother disciplined me for yelling and being disrespectful in her house, but I knew I had hurt him with my words, and in a twisted way, I had some satisfaction knowing that. I knew it was wrong, but it was how I honestly felt. During this whole time, we still attended church services regularly, as a family, minus my stepfather.

So, when I mentioned that growing up in the Church had its blessings and curses earlier, here is an example of what I meant. "*How does a child process the living situation they are in and obey what God commands without being taught how?*" That event traumatized me, even though I know it was not my fault. I struggled with following the dictates of the Bible, where it says for me to "*Love your enemies.*" I often wondered how am I to do that? Knowing what the Bible says, and doing it, identified the gap in my Christian learning. I was taught about Jesus in Sunday school and learned the principles of Christianity while still living in a home with the person responsible for the trauma I experienced. It was complicated to say the least. Listen, parents and guardians, the life issues do not go away because you try to pick up the pieces and keep living. There were undeniable fears, anger, and resentment built up that required healing. When the emotional stuff is not dealt with, the most respectful and obedient children may harbor ill feelings towards themselves and find themselves only existing, but not truly living. At least, that is what happened to me.

I can only speak for myself; however, I know my brother processed it differently. I cannot say how it has fully affected and impacted his life. Only he can do that. Early in building a relationship with Jesus and learning about Him, I believed my mother loved my stepfather more than she loved us. I know now this was a lie from the pit of hell; and it was part of my mental perception of my life at that time. I was becoming a teenager with raging hormones and unstable emotions.

The enemy of my soul wanted to take me out early in life. What he failed to understand is he cannot stop the intents and purposes of God. So, he took an unexpected approach. He distracted me with the issues of life that flowed out of my heart (Proverbs 4:21). He attempted to get me to reject God's will for my life. However, it only delayed God's plans for my life while he attempted to destroy me during the delay. Satan did not care if I knew my purpose, or even if I accepted it. His mission was to keep me from fulfilling my purpose and completing the goals associated with it. The moment I surrendered to God and submitted to His will, He empowered me to destroy every word and work of the enemy, with Jesus as my example. It did not mean Satan stopped or gave up trying to deceive me. On the contrary, he seemed to have upped his game and began going after the people closest to me.

The Sunday after my big blow-up, we went to church, and the pastor preached a sermon on forgiveness and said, 'do not have alt in your heart.' He also said we should forgive so that we are not forever separated from Jesus. I believed enough in Jesus to know I did not want to be separated forever from Him. After I obtained a thirteen-year-old understanding of forgiveness and unforgiveness, I had to ask my stepfather for forgiveness, and I did not know how or when to do it. The fear and thought of being separated from Jesus, the One who holds the entire world in His hands and the One before I prayed to before I ate, and who I learned loves me while in Sunday school. It bothered me to think I would not be with Him forever. I knew it was necessary to forgive. It was Father's Day when I decided to give him a forgiveness letter before we left for Church. In that letter, I shared with him I forgave him for his part in the traumatic event I experienced, and that I was sorry for saying I hated him. It would be the first of many times I had to ask for forgiveness from the people in my life. For me, that moment was pivotal, because I wanted to please God, rather than be separated from him while holding the anger, hurt, pride and unforgiveness in my heart and mind. I acknowledged my sin, hurt, anger, and confusion in my desire to please God. I knew in my heart that I needed to ask for forgiveness, and when I did, things in our household changed. I learned a valuable lesson that the enemy fights against obedience to God, because it puts the believer in alignment with God, and highlights the fact that God's power and His word are our best defense.

The enemy of our soul has no power or defense greater than the Almighty God. I had to learn forgiveness early in life. I developed a distrust of my father figures early in my life, and thought my mom was a drill sergeant who taught obedience, structure, and boundaries with discipline. The enemy of my soul played on my immature mind and my unstable emotions by convincing me that my family rejected me. By the time I turned fourteen, the rejection and fear that started at age five had taken root and grew into a stronghold in my life. To add to an already struggling teenager, I am now entering high school, having a debilitating identity crisis, experiencing peer pressure, being bullied, becoming a bully, encountering new people who influenced my life, experiencing yet another new school, and the continuous family drama and issues at home; all were infecting, affecting, and impacting my life during my first year of high school. It was hard to adjust to it all! I know what you are thinking, in 2020 it is far worse. I am not comparing war stories, but even with everything I went through in my young life, this current generation has seen and done things I never encountered in school or at home. There is a more excellent call on parents, guardians, and/or authority figures to connect with their younger self to help today's youth endure what they face by giving and showing more love and understanding. Plato said, *"Kindness is more than deeds. It is an attitude, an expression, a look, a touch. It is anything that lifts another person."* Robin Williams said, *"Everyone you meet is fighting a battle you know nothing about. Be kind. Always."*

In high school, I was athletic and on the track team. We went to the state competition my freshman year, and during that meet, I had a few new encounters that formed my high school experience. My hormones were in high effect! I had a crush on a sophomore from a rival school. We talked on the phone all the time, and because he showed me attention and said he loved me, I fell hard for him. Was it love? I thought so! I was so naive when I imagined I would marry him one day simply because he showed me the attention I craved, and I believed he accepted me. I wanted a male's love so badly. Especially since my biological father and my stepfather did not seem to love me. We were like two magnets quickly being pulled into a universe that I created in my mind. As our relationship developed, I believed he loved me. I was so young and foolish to the motives and intents of young teenage boys. As you would expect, our emotional connection led to a physical relationship.

In my mind, he would marry me and take me away from my home, and we would live happily ever after. I soon learned this was a fairy tale because that never happened! Our love was merely a figment of my imagination!!! Before summer vacation was over, he had convinced me he loved me and that we should express our mutual love during intercourse. I lost my virginity to him, and a month later, I found out I was pregnant at age fifteen. Another life-changing event, except this time it brought shame and horrific fears that compounded my other concerns. I was a teenager! I did not know how to be a mother. This caused me to become so emotionally distraught that I contemplated suicide to get relief from the torture I experienced from the shame I brought to me and my family.

In my mind, I caused every family issue, and wanted to become invisible. I went through cycles of guilt, shame, and fear that seemed to add to the concerns and rejection already present in my life. I was a mess. Although my mother and stepfather helped me by supporting me as best they could, I felt like a tremendous burden, and I was at a horrendously low place in my life. My self-esteem and self-worth were at its lowest. My unstable mental condition, my surging hormones, and my pregnancy caused me to feel even more rejected my father figures, my mother, and other family members. On one of my darkest days, I had an aunt come to visit and talk with me. She looked me in the eye, something I did not do from shame, and encouraged me. She told me that God loves me and that she loves me too. She told me not to quit or give up, and that I could still graduate high school and continue my life. I deeply appreciated her words and the love she showed me during her visit, but I could not process any of what she said to me.

All I could see was the continuous building of rejection, fear, anger, bitterness, resentment, and rebellion in me. Now I am more confused than ever because I thought life was supposed to be good with Jesus, but that was not the case in my house! Even as I write this, I know that many children have suffered much worse problems than the events that took place in my life, but I can say to them that there is hope, love and peace in Jesus. I encourage anyone experiencing emotional, physical, and/or mental pain to go to a teacher, counselor, trusted family member, and/or other trustworthy people for help. Do not try to cope on your own! It only leads to you making horrible decisions, believing you are all alone, and doing whatever is necessary to survive!

Whether you are young, old, or anywhere in between, making impulsive, reactive, and/or hurried decisions can set you up for unnecessary pain. Many life-altering tragedies cannot be adverted in life, but in those moments when you hear there is a better way to live, believe it. It was during those moments that I believe God gives you hope to come through and/or overcome the most trying times in your life.

When you or I read the Word of God, it points out our sins and how we are out of alignment with God's will for our life and provides the instructions on how to get into alignment with God's will. It is the reader's choice to obey what God has said or not. Understanding that both decisions carry consequences, good and bad. While identifying the sins in my life, God opened my release moments to receive His forgiveness. Learning to forgive set me up for deliverance, healing, and/or being released from the many issues in my life. I had to decide whether to obey God wholeheartedly and understand His will as my way of life, or to continue being rebellious, stubborn, and disobedient while suffering the knocks and hits from those actions.

The importance of obedience to my Heavenly Father through Christ Jesus offered me the opportunity to use the power of the Holy Spirit as I continued to obey Him and follow His instructions. Those negative actions of disobedience did not bring the desired change into my life. However, once I released my control to God and obeyed Him and remain obedient, change became apparent not only in my life but also in lives I influenced.

I existed, but never dealt with my hurt, fears, and mental wounds from my teen pregnancy. I continued to be low key in activities other than church, family and/or holiday related activities due to the shame I felt. I continued to excel in high school and graduated on time. By the time I graduated from high school, I was afraid of what the next chapter in my life would look like. I was a teen mother accepted into a university in another city in my state, and I had never left home before. I was afraid of leaving my child, thinking she might forget me, and leaving my family. No matter how dysfunctional my family was, they were still my family! What was I supposed to do without having them around me? All that, plus insecurity, low self-esteem, poor self-image, and uncertainty about the success of my college experience, plagued my mind constantly. How could I do the new and unknown by myself? Was I even worthy of going to college? After praying and accepting this as my reality, my answer was yes! I worked hard, so I could go to this university, but I did not know how to function in this new experience? I thought merely three years ago; I was the girl who would do nothing with her life but make babies and live on welfare. As I reflected, I remember the times I overheard people predict my future and write me off because I had become a teen mom. My mother always spoke life into me and told me I was going to be something. Even when I was pregnant, she told me I was going to graduate high school with my class, and I did exactly that with honors.

If I had known then how my mother would step up and be a catalyst in the life of my future self, I might not have had such a difficult time with the various transitions I experienced in life. Meaning if I had heard more affirmations of positive things in my life, I may have believed in my potential.

As a freshman in high school with raging hormones, it made me vulnerable to the lust of the flesh, and the lies this young man used to get what he wanted from me. I cannot put all the blame on him because I allowed it. However, God took that negative, turned it into a positive, and used it to save my life. I endured the shame, fear, and guilt. There were even times when I wanted to commit suicide. The embarrassment I experienced at Church, compiled with the shame, guilt and fear of this pregnancy, put me mentally in a place where I believed suicide was the answer to the issue before me. But

God would not allow that to be the ending to my story. Instead, He taught me how to rewrite my story while teaching me how to live a victorious life.

I had an aunt who encouraged me, and Mothers of the Church, who encouraged me and offered hope. My mother told me I was going to still succeed in life and finish high school, but I could not understand how it was possible. I had a maternal grandmother who prayed for me. I am here to let you know that the prayers of the righteous 'availeth much.' I did not die, but lived to declare the works of the Lord, Hallelujah!

In this stage of life, I had to take responsibility for my thoughts and actions. I could not make excuses but learn to repent and live through the hardship and shame. I did not have a person teaching me this directly, but God was building me into a vessel of notable character from the many times I sat on the potter's wheel. He purified me for His glory and let others know that my story is neither ideal nor pretty, but it is real and a testimony to the greatness of God's power.

I learned I ate way too much of the wrong things emotionally and/or spiritually that ended up affecting my natural appetite. I ate too much television, which led to an overactive imagination. Later in life, the reality that what I manifested was nothing like my fantasy life. You know the one in my mind. I ate fairytales and fake news. I bet many can relate, but I am so glad this is not the end of my story. It was merely laying the groundwork. Transformation can only occur when we admit something is wrong in our lives. It happens when we know that things must change, even when we do not know how they will change.

For example, I thought I would marry my first boyfriend and live happily ever after. However, my reality was that God knew that the child I was carrying had a purpose, just like each human being has. Jesus paid the price for all my sins to be forgiven, but I had to repent of my sins and receive the forgiveness. I could not accept God's forgiveness until after I learned to forgive myself, and that took a long time. I can now understand how God started that process. I had to fail in life, experience some devastating mental battles, fall down, be humbled, get up and fall down some more from age 15 to thirty-two, before clarity and spiritual grounding as a believer manifested differently in my life. I learned God did not condemn me. He redeemed me with the blood Jesus shed on Calvary's cross. Yes, my sins had consequences when I did not repent! However, when I repented, the blood of Jesus completed its perfect work in my life that no one can ever change.

Learning became the alternate universe I escaped to. It took me away from the issues at home and the awkwardness of growing up. My only focus became getting good grades. I lacked social skills and self-confidence. I failed to see myself in a positive light. Everything about me was a no! Charisma, no! Good looks, no! At least in my eyes. As if what I was dealing with was not enough!

Before graduating, I met a young man who became my high school sweetheart. He took me to the senior prom, and we continued to see each other after I graduated. The thought of leaving him for college was heartbreaking. To add more heartache and stress to my decision, I was leaving home for the first time, leaving my daughter in the care of my mother and step-dad, and leaving my brother. As I reflect on this memory, it was the first time my brother and I were ever separated. As I opened new doors to have new experiences, he entered puberty and tried to figure out who he is. I remember being socially awkward, shy, and scared. I was forced to adapt to all the changes occurring in my life simultaneously. In my first year of college, I focused on my coursework and my work-study job. It allowed me to send money home to my parents to help with my daughter. That year, I learned responsibility, time management, and how to get good grades. I was so homesick. I visited home every opportunity I got. I would go home every break, and as expected it affected my concentration and grades.

As I got used to college life and its nightlife, I started being exposed to Greek life, their parties, alcohol, and its promiscuous sexual activity. Although I am not proud of the things I participated in while at university, it is part of my story and reality. When I was nineteen, I found out I was pregnant with my second child, and the university informed my parents. I hit rock bottom. I was afraid of what they would think of me, and here I am again, bringing shame upon my family. Another pregnancy, and I am still not married. The pressure I was under, the depression I dealt with, and the shame I experienced were overwhelming, and once again, I contemplated suicide. In my depressed and stressed-out mind, I believed I could take a paycheck and pay for an abortion. It would solve everything, but I could not follow through with it. I know it was God speaking to my heart not to kill this innocent life. God helped me comprehend my child has a purpose and would give me more than I ever gave him/her. I just could not kill my baby. With all the stuff going on in my head and heart, I could not concentrate on my coursework, and I flunked out. I returned home pregnant and ashamed. Although I worked and contributed to our household, I always felt a thick cloud of shame sitting heavily over my life. There became a time when the family of my baby's father asked if the child was his. Especially since they knew I was away at college when I got pregnant. Their opinion of me had changed, and it created stress in our relationship. Here we go again! I am faced with another group of people who dislike me and judge me. For reasons, I cannot fathom, they believed I was trying to trap their loved one.

Take a step back in time with me to the latter part of my caterpillar stage. Now I am a sophomore in high school and a teen mother. My first daughter was born healthy and beautiful, and I learned I could not live for myself because a life depended on my life choices and decisions. I began to mature quickly with that in mind. God allowed her to be born to save my life. I began praying and reading more about the Jesus I had been taught in Sunday school. I needed Him to be my Lord and teach me how to live my life. I did not know it then, but my daughter would be a catalyst for me to pray more and ask God to help me be a good mother to this innocent life. No book, but the Bible could provide me with the instructions I needed to live my very real life. You see, I had low self-esteem, shame, embarrassment, and self-hatred, which I wore like a layer of clothing. But God! God used this season to teach me to have faith, believe in the healing powers of His love through Jesus, and that my current situation did not define me. It was only a chapter in the story of my life. I used to sing the song Jesus loves me this I know, and during this stage of life I believed it. I was shown God's great love through the men and women who lived God's Love before me. No matter what stage of life you may be at, are you watching what you are eating? You should! It affects your physical, mental, and spiritual wellness in your body. At least it did in my life!

I graduated from High School and entered a new phase in my relationship with my high school sweetheart. Two weeks after turning eighteen, I was leaving home for the first time to go to college. In the first year, I was an exemplary student, working, learning, and growing in responsibility. But the insecurities, missing home and missing my high school sweetheart, started a chain of events I was not prepared to handle or foresaw. The summer after my first year of college, my sweetheart and I decided we were ready to start an intimate relationship. Well, we were not for many reasons, but we acted upon what we thought was love. Two months into my second year of college, I found out I was pregnant. Now, after all I experienced at fifteen, I should have made wiser choices, I know! The college notified my parents, and I tried to run from my life, but couldn't. So, I maintained excellent grades until the second semester. Shame and fear again plagued me, and I decided to party in the fraternities with two new best friends: Mad Dog 20/20, and Wild Irish Rose alcoholic beverages. In an attempt to avoid, deny, and hide, I was a sophomore in college and pregnant by my high school sweetheart. I am flunking out of college, bringing more shame to my family, and soon I would be back home with my parents, who were taking care of my first child. My high school sweetheart knew it was his child, but his family thought I was trapping him with our individual and collective irresponsible actions. He never denied me or my pregnancy. He took full responsibility and accepted the criticism that came along with being an unwed/teen parent with me. At age 19, my second child was born healthy and unaffected by my brief time with my previous best friends. We made plans to get married because we knew it was the right thing to do. A little more life happened, and I became pregnant by Him again, and at age twenty, we welcomed another baby girl into our lives.

My life had become a discretionary tale that informed onlookers to wait until they are married to have sex. I saw myself as the black sheep of our family, and that perception created a whole new dynamic in our household. It became a place of stress, shame, and disappointment for me. I now realize it was one of my own making. The day I heard a family member say I will end up with a bunch of kids and on welfare for the rest of my life changed my life. The cut from their words were so deep it motivated me to prove them wrong. I worked hard to care for and raise my children. I was not lazy nor wanted handouts. Even though I contributed to the household by working and raising my children, I never realized how the comments of the people closest to my parents brought them grief, because they helped support me and my children.

From the negative comments made by some family members, I kept my distance. I did not want to overhear or subject myself to their prediction of who I would become. Especially when I became pregnant with child number three. While pregnant with her, I experienced some life-threatening health issues. When I was seven months pregnant, I had an emergency appendectomy, and a month later, I was back in the hospital. This time for a month with pneumonia. While in the hospital, my left lung collapsed, and I had a tough road to recovery from these health issues and my pregnancy. As if everything else I was dealing with was not enough, I went past my delivery date, and the doctor induced labor. During the delivery, the baby got stuck in the birth canal, and I had an emergency cesarean section. Even with all the health issues I had during my pregnancy, she was born bright-eyed and healthy in February, 1992. In July of the same year, I married the love of my life and my best friend. That one act dispelled many of the statements made by family members due to the children I birthed outside of marriage.

My husband and I worked hard and saved for our wedding, honeymoon, and two months' rent for our new apartment. After two months of married life, we were greeted with a surprise! We were pregnant with child number four. My husband wanted a boy who would carry his name. Thankfully, God granted his request because this was my last child, whether male or female, as far as I was concerned. Our son arrived on schedule in April, 1993, one month before my twenty-second birthday. At this juncture in my life, I am a twenty-two-year-old married woman, mother of four, working full time, maintaining our home, and handling the responsibilities with my husband and all it entailed. I am evolving into a mature woman, and I am loving my life. But deep down, I had a yearning that would not go away. I wanted to finish college and get the degree I did not get while at the university. I wanted better career opportunities to support our family.

There was so much that happened in the third set of seven years of life that impacted my ability to judge manipulation and control the tactics used by family members and/or other authoritative figures in my life. All of which played a significant role in the development of the people-pleasing-coping mechanism I used to deal with my need to be accepted by people. All of which were a by-product of having children out of wedlock. In my mind, if I did well in school, it showed my intelligence. However, it was never celebrated, only tolerated because someone would inevitably say, "If she is so smart, then why does she keep having babies while living at home?" I needed people to recognize how hard I worked at being responsible as an escape from the people who did nothing but bring up how much I owed them for their help. They would say things like '…if they did not have to help me, they could have more money, cars, etc.' My rejection riddled mind, interpreted their comments and superior attitudes as me being a burden! It made me believe I needed to hurry up and leave my parent's home, so they did not have to support and/or help me anymore. It was not like I did not accept my wrongdoing or acknowledge what I needed to do to make things right. My guilt created a scenario where it was acceptable for me to endure criticism while being committed to pleasing and/or appeasing them until I could live on my own.

During this time, I learned a lot about the people surrounding me: those who judged me, those who openly spoke death over my life with their assumptions about me, and those who I knew loved me. I carried the weight of the world on my shoulders and in my mind. I also learned a lot about myself. I had no clue how to build a loving and lasting relationship. They believed I was reckless and loose. When, in fact, I was committed to living and doing better to communicate with my husband. He was my confidant and the holder of my secrets. We seemed to gravitate to each other because we both had family issues. We built our relationship from our mutual need to help each other through our tough times and challenging days. Especially when dealing with our individual families. That mindset and those behaviors appeared to further inflame my belief that "Everything that went wrong in my household was my fault!" The sad thing about it all is there was always someone around who reminded me of that very thing. Whenever my achievements were recognized, I was often reminded I needed to focus on working and contributing to the house, because I am the reason there is never enough money in the household.

For seven years, I struggled with my need to win the approval of and be accepted by people, especially the people who made up my family. The very people who shunned me, unless it benefited them. I wish I were exaggerating, but when you are fed lies and believe them, it governs how you live. I was fighting an unbeatable battle in the sense that I could not change anyone's mind regarding me. I could only change my perception of myself and the reality in which I existed. In my state of mind, I honestly believed I had let God down... I had let my family down, and I brought shame to them by my actions. My choices had consequences. They treated me differently at Church. I could not associate with my cousins because my aunts thought I might influence them to have sex and get pregnant. Five or six years later, those same cousins got pregnant, and you will never guess what happened. I was called to my aunt's houses and accused of knowing about their pregnancies. I was told I needed to talk to them. Now, these are the same aunts who refused to allow me to have any contact with my cousins outside of encountering them at Church and at some family gatherings. Now they wanted me to talk to them. When I tell you, people can throw you under the bus, backup, and roll over you again just to make sure you are dead. That was equivalent to what was happening here. They accused me of having more influence than I ever believed. Somehow, I had influenced all the innocent teen girls in the congregation, the ones I was not allowed to talk to or interact with, simply from them knowing I was an unwed mother. None of my accomplishments meant anything. The fact that I got married and was raising my children did not change their opinion of me. It was only because of God that I made it through that experience, and so many others, with some semblance of sanity. The emotional turmoil I experienced, the accusations I endured, and the ridicule I suffered through... it is a wonder I am still in the land of the living. For reasons, I cannot explain, I accepted the responsibilities forced upon me by my aunts and the people at Church because I bought into the lie the enemy of my soul told me. I allowed my emotions to lead me, and wore the shame, guilt, and fear as my protective covering, and allowed it to become my place of escape. Even when hurt and anger were added to the emotions I wore daily, I never lashed out at anyone who spoke this non-sense to me. I internalized it because I did not know how to release it and because I would never disrespect an adult. I accepted each word as truth because they were grown... they knew better... they were correct, right?

As I compare the transformational stages of a butterfly to my life, I have recognized my growth, failures, how I overcame situations designed to destroy me, and empowered to be here today. As I share my journey of truth, I realize I am not alone on this earth, and that there are specific lives who will gain clarity, strength, and comfort from the experiences I share. I have experienced several life situations I do not cover in this book. What I have done is to obey God and share the areas that were the most traumatic to me. Whatever God you see in and through my life, know it was from my transformation by God's Holy Spirit that has empowered me to live when the natural thing would be to die to escape the pain before tapping into my potential. I challenge you to let "Release Moments" bring clarity to how God taught me to forgive, strengthened me with His Word to overcome situations, restrictions, and even myself. God's word has empowered me to fight and live, not only for me, but also for everyone attached, connected, assigned, and purposed to interact with or be in relationship with me.

The importance of this background information is to show what caused me to seek God to heal me of my past, receive forgiveness for my sins and offer forgiveness to myself.

Look at what I ate naturally, spiritually, and mentally. Look at what my choices and actions produced. Look at the near-death experience encountered to bring forth a life. Even in all I have gone through, I can still see the hand of God moving, rearranging, and orchestrating my life. God changed the trajectory of the life events that should have killed me to build me. I know how to master academic systems because I love to learn. I have two bachelor's degrees, one master's degree, and am working on a second master's degree. My life testifies that although I can learn the world system and achieve worldly knowledge, God had to humble me to learn the spiritual knowledge needed to submit and experience change in my life. In all honesty, it was easier to learn the world's system than to have faith and live in God's system.

Remember, at this point, I am now married to my high school sweetheart and am the mother of our three children. In September 1992, we found out I was expecting our fourth child. Behold, my life is littered with the mess-ups I did before. So, I thought, before I got it right. But if NO HUMAN pats you on the back because you choose to stand for God, make sure God has your back and that He strengthenss you to obey, love, and follow Him above all else. People often say you are so wise, but you weren't in the dark place with me when I was foolish and got chastised by God. Some people say you are so thoughtful, but you were not there when I was so wrapped up in myself that I acted selfishly. God would convict, chastise, rebuke, and offer me the choice to obey or disobey, while telling me what I choose will determine how I will reap the benefit or consequence. I went from Church to a local assembly building and learned how to teach others the lessons I learned in creative ways. I went from shame to sharing with others how telling your truth, being obedient to God's word and will for your life will produce in you the strength you need to overcome those things designed to destroy your hope and kill your joy. The only way this happened was by the power of God, through His Holy Spirit.

CHAPTER 3: Learning Through the Process of My Mess

Pupa is the next stage in the butterfly's development. This is where the caterpillar creates a cocoon for cell transformation to occur. Well, my life from ages twenty-two to twenty-eight speaks of how I was socially, physically, and spiritually cocooned. Let me explain. I am a newlywed, mother of four, and had my son with no pain medication. My husband prayed for and wanted our son to be an heir to the family name. A year later, I am working full-time and taking everything; I learned from my childhood, teens, and young adult years to learn how to be a good wife. Keep in mind, I had dysfunctional models until this point. It was like I pieced my perception of the women in my life in their proper positions and sought to make it part of me. I repeated the same process with other people's lives I had access to and surmised if I do this or that I will be a wonderful mother, Church member, and/or supportive wife. Therefore, I had to be cocooned, because God had to transform me completely from looking at the perfectly flawed models of women I honored and loved. God had to show me He made me to be Rosetta and gave Jesus as the example of how to live obediently while honoring God. What God taught me during my cocoon stage was that I cannot do everything everyone else is doing. Change had to occur in me for me to see myself the way God created, designed, and purposed me to be identified.

At age twenty-seven, God put a desire and fire in me to share with youth the experiences I have lived, and teach God's Word, His will, and way while being transparent, so they would be prepared for the real-life changes that will occur when a believer sins against God's Word. I know I was not ideal, worthy, or qualified, but God chose me to be transformed, help bring transformation in love, truth, and commitment to the youth He sends to me. It became another way God brought change into my life and to share the message of change with others. I pray if you are in your cocoon stage, the pupa stage, and God separates you despite your life situations, know that you are in good company with remarkable men like Abraham, Moses, and David, just to name a few. In my cocoon, I learned that death had to happen so that God's life can begin in me. Listen, I did not do it perfectly. I did it faithfully.

While creating this youth ministry, which included my children and other members of the congregation's children, and even neighborhood youth, I understood God's purpose is to impact generations. God brought my life full circle. The hurt, shame, pain, perceived rejection, and unresolved spiritual void are now instruments of growth for me and the youth I teach. I learned how to surrender in that cocoon, and the importance of daily surrendering to the will and way of God. I often prayed for insight to be authentic, creative, and helpful to the youth. I learned to be the help I did not have when transitioning through various stages of life. I would speak the truth about sin, hell, obedience, and heaven. And I could not make their choices, but I could be a godly influence for them to help them make better decisions than I did. Did this always work? No! But the work is still necessary. Every time God taught me a godly principle, He would give me an acronym, phrase, or song to make the lessons understandable for the youth in the program. Even though I was in a cocoon, I was being used to plant godly seeds in youth that others could water, and at the proper time, there would be a harvest.

When telling some of my release moments, I would revisit the emotions and thoughts I felt. God had to remind me that hurt people hurt people; but more importantly, healed people heal people. God's Spirit had to show me how to stop looking at the negatives in my life moments and praise Him. I had time to repent, turn away from my sins, and receive healing. God was putting me through the paces of a spiritual boot camp, so that as I was healed, I was immediately put in a position to show someone else the process. Yes, each person can admit they have had horrific moments, but then reflect on how God moved in you and through you during those moments. It is amazing how you can give God a mighty testimony despite what happened to you.

Did you get broken to get put back together? And who can you help you share your testimony? How has God delivered you? Do you still need deliverance? Are you willing to allow God to deliver you?

I have so many learning experiences that have humbled me and taught me how to be obedient to God's word. I rarely hear people give their full testimony of the hurt, shame and ugly He brought them through. It is the same with the struggles they consistently endured, and their embarrassment when seeking others for prayer, confession, and/or to be a port in the storms of life. It would have helped me understand not everyone is perfect in their Christian walk. They struggled in the same way that I was struggling, because we are all imperfect. God processed me through my chastisement, and equipped me to tell my entire story, not merely the best and/or pleasing parts. There are young adults yearning for Jesus, but are repulsed by the religious traditions or modern services that present a graceful, always contented life when they are living toilsome days. All Christians should be ready to explain why they believe, and unashamedly share how God transformed their life so they can live righteously today. I am not perfect, and that was not God's requirement, but I had to be taught how to be holy and righteous. Time and time again, I was stubborn. God had to whip me into shape. I learned how to use the tools He shared with me to bask in and live in the love, obedience, holiness, and righteousness He offers. I learned to tell my truth and share the Christians principals that have worked in my life. I did not know how to work out my soul's salvation, and from zero to twenty-eight, I was unknowingly being prepared for the cocoon stage God used to transform me. Now, I can share with others the love, care, hope, and grace God brought into my life that changed the ending to my story. I learned how to be honest and pliable for God to teach me how to live the Bible principles, rightly divide the word of truth and teach it to others. It offered hope to the hearers to know that their lives would not be in the dark to the truth of God's will. Even when they do not obey the Bible, I had to accept them where they are, pray and love them to life. I could not leave them in their sin. I was charged to help them along their way, because that is exactly what God did for me.

God saw me in my cocoon! God had to help me stop avoiding the painful areas of my life, give a voice to my hurt and pain, and allow Him to heal me. It was transformational because when you have run from the unpleasant moments for so long as I did, fear and shame prevent you from facing them. But God!

I stopped blaming my parents, stepfather, and/or everyone I believed were responsible for my current predicament, because it was easier to lie down and be the victim instead of standing up and being the victor! I was not fighting for myself. I had four children with all this mighty potential, which required me to submit to God to be the example in their home of someone who followed God, not merely at the Church, but in every area of life. It evolved into a lifestyle. I believed Jesus won the victory for every Christian, but I had to win the victory in my mind and heart to experience His healing power and allow Him to exchange my stony heart for a fleshly one made soft by His love. I learned I could trust God! No matter how many times I failed, He would pick me up, dust me off, and love me back to life. God showed me my greatest ministry was to be with my husband and children. God healed me to be the conduit He uses to give them the tools that I wish I had growing up to live righteously and authentically. I could never make their decisions for them, but I can prepare them to make better decisions during key moments in life. God transformed me to break me, free me, and empower me to share my powerful testimony.

The childhood events that were outside my control both affected and infected me in ways only God can understand. He took those infections of pain, traumas, guilt, and shame, and changed them into opportunities to affect a change in me and through me to impact others' lives. I turned inward and expressed anger and hatred towards myself. That is why when God transformed me while reading His Word, correcting me while teaching me obedience to His Word, and healing the deep-seated mental and spiritual wounds, it makes me eternally grateful for my release moments. Humans are flawed, and the best Christians will fail to live up to people's expectations of them. However, God takes us as we are, and His love patches up our wounds, breaths love into our broken hearts, and offers the peace that surpasses all understanding as we step into who we are purposed to be. When I got married, I had all this mental, emotional, and spiritual baggage I carried around. I did not have a therapist or counselor to help me unpack my baggage and release it. I lived daily with the shame, hurtful words, and judgmental attitudes I experienced while growing up. If I am being brutally honest, not all of it came from outside sources. Most of it was coming from within me and justified the story I told myself. It is amazing that I did not have a breakdown or ended up in a mental hospital from the stress and pressure I put on myself. God strategically orchestrated outlets for me that provided "…a way to escape, that [I could] bear…" (1 Corinthians 10:13) the negatives thrown at me that allowed me to focus on something positive instead. My mother put me in programs that gave affirmations I did not receive from those closest to me.

One such program was the Center for Leadership Development (CLD). I was a graduate of the class of 1988 and was taught by Mr. Bundles. It was and still is today one of the finest organizations I could ever be part of. It was during my tenure at CLD that a mind shift happened, and I began thinking differently. One of the highlights for me was when I won an award from Ball State for my high school grades. For the first time in my life, someone outside my family recognized my grades. I thought my family would be proud of my accomplishments, but they were NOT proud of me! They were only proud that I did well, if that makes sense. There was no show of affection or even excitement. Do not get me wrong, I knew my mom and stepdad loved me from their commitment to providing me with shelter, food, clothes, and shoes. Even when money was low, the needs of both my brother and I were met. I recognized it as a blessing then, just as I do now. There were few emotions shown by the women in my life. They taught the girls to be tough, and the boys were protected because they could easily be killed. I am not saying it was right or wrong. What I am saying is it was an unspoken rule. Whether it was verbalized or shown in the actions and attitudes of those around me, it was there lurking in the shadows of my life. There came a point in my marriage, maybe four and a half years in, when me and my husband's individual family issues came to a head and had to be dealt with because we had no desire to be like our parents hiding secrets and/or avoiding issues.

It was painful to reveal my true heart about the family shaming I experienced to my husband. As a woman, a black woman at that, there is a double standard. I do not know how many times I heard, "Momma's baby, Daddy's maybe," and since I was not denying my children or their father, that statement offended me. I took my responsibility as a mother seriously because the role was not an option for me. I was strict, organized, and orderly while raising our children! I believed that by thinking that way, I could control the environment my children lived in to keep them safe while we provided for them. If I could not control something, I would avoid it or remove it from my life. I did not see a need to change it because it was what I saw in my household growing up. It was normal, right? Eventually, I learned an invaluable lesson; how can a man be a man if you are trying to be the man for him? OUCH!!!! Listen, we had some healing to do, individually and as a couple. Once I recognized what I was doing was incorrect, I learned how to be a wife, and I released those things that no longer served me, so I could raise my children as God intended. My husband and I were both raised in Church. We knew who Jesus was, but we had a significant amount of growing to do to develop a personal relationship with Him. In the early years of our marriage, the principles of our faith instilled in us while growing up were our saving grace. Especially on those days when being married was a challenge.

A Breakthrough Release Moment: My Heart Revealed

Ages twenty-two through twenty-eight were pivotal years for me. I discovered I was merely existing and not truly living. At my core, I am a responsible, loving woman who housed self-doubt in my heart and mind from the many unresolved issues leftover from my childhood. I remember discussing the future of our family with my husband, and we came up with a game plan. While he went to technical school to become an automotive technician, I started working two jobs to support our family. After eight months of living this lifestyle, I almost had a stroke. I had a blood vessel burst in my eye from insufficient sleep and burning the candle at both ends. Working and taking care of our children and household while balancing the family's Church activities became overwhelming. It started off okay, and I believed I could handle it. That is, until it became too much. The health scare made me stop and re-evaluate my life! I thought about what I needed, who I loved, etc. During this time, I sought God, as I never did before. I quickly realized my life depended on the guidance I got from Him.

While transitioning from my teens into my twenties, I began transitioning through many phases in my life. From the unplanned pregnancies to the emotional trauma I experienced at the hands of the people closest to me, I realized I had not dealt with the issues of my childhood. I thought I had, but I had stuffed them and worked extremely hard to not allow them to show up in my reality. Most of my issues in life were mental issues, centered around my thinking patterns, my way of being overly critical of myself, and our marriage became a reflection of my embedded thoughts. I allowed other's opinions, negative words, and disrespect to become major hinderances and stumbling blocks in my life. I bought into the lies of the enemy hook, line, and sinker! I believed I had no significant self-worth, and the lies about my abilities and/or capabilities. I believed that if I excelled in my academics, I was successful. I compared that to my belief that I was unsuccessful in any other area of my life. Of course, that was not true! Keep in mind, I am setting the stage for you to understand where I was mentally and emotionally. God showed me the motive behind every decision I made was the idea that I did not want to repeat the cycle of getting right to the edge of a breakthrough and falling back into my self-sabotaging ways. Instead of moving forward, I was going backwards and coming upon the point of no return. At least that is what I thought. The mental anguish I experienced became a stronghold in my life from which I needed deliverance. I intentionally fasted and prayed for the deliverance I sought. When I was delivered, I developed a strategy to move forward that took both courage and determination not to be a victim, but a victor in my life by the power of God.

I once believed that with academics, I could accomplish anything because I had done it many times in my life. However, God gave me business ideas, hopes and dreams for my future, and aspirations to venture out into new territories of possibilities, but I saw them as impossibilities because I relied on my knowledge, strength, and resources instead of trusting God. Today I realize I missed opportunities that will not come around again. How I look at that entire scenario today matters because I learned how to trust God and believe what He said, instead of being consumed by my self-doubts and the lies told by the enemy of my soul. What is shocking now, but was a way of life back then, was when I would create scenarios that hindered my progress, because I could not see any proof that what I was being shown was possible. I was looking to those around me for validation and/or confirmation for what can only be found in myself and in God. I realize all this now, but back then I was involved in spiritual warfare and did not know it. Most of my life, I heard nothing but negativity except in school. God placed teachers and school adjuncts in my life who encouraged and gave me the tools and skills to think past my current state in life and dream! I am grateful to each of them for what they poured into me. At one point in my life, I tried to be who I believed others perceived/expected me to be, rather than learning how to be me and make that enough! I am a purposed vessel for God's glory, born to do good works that God prepared for me before the foundation of the world was ever created, or as Jeremiah 1:5 says, "*Before I formed thee in the belly, I knew thee; and before thou camest forth out of the womb, I sanctified thee, and I ordained thee…*"

No one, including me, is perfect! Therefore, I am not blaming anyone for the events of my life. I am sharing the truth of my journey through life. I learned that God would make me face intolerable situations in life, and as He guided me through those moments, He wanted me to show someone else how He brought me through. Usually, I had to fast, pray, dig deep in the Bible, and use the word of God to break through situations. The hard way was and is my journey. The lies I listened to and believed over the truth of God's word, and the possibilities of my life were holding me hostage. It took me a long time to wrap my mind around being loved and accepted by God, because certain people in my life were used by the enemy of my soul to make me feel worthless and undeserving! At some point in my life, each of the rejections from people made me draw into God, and yes, I was an emotional wreck, but God kept me. I had family and Church members who made it appear they were perfect at everything, and life was simply wonderful. They had me believing everything I did was horrible, and it messed me up for many years. From ages fifteen to twenty-three, I was constantly fighting to keep my mind, because subconsciously I believed the lies. I tried to change my self-sabotaging behavior, only to find myself drawn back into that pattern of thinking over and over again. God had to remind me that He is my source of strength and power. I see now that faulty thinking played into my job choices, as well. I had multiple jobs where I worked hard and was given opportunities to advance because I had outstanding leadership skills and positively influenced my co-workers. I did not take advantage of them because I did not believe I was supervisor or management material because I did not have a degree. I turned down those opportunities from a fear of failing. Rather than trying I stayed at the level I was because it was familiar! As they say the devil you know is better than the devil you do not know! I always seemed to reject management's assessment of me because I could not see what they saw. I thought it was a trick to get me in a vulnerable position so they could make a fool of me. Anyone who knew me knew I was not going out like that.

I thought I was protecting myself from other people's actions. I needed to control the people, places and things that impacted and/or intersected with my life. As long as I could control my surroundings, I felt safe from the hurt inflicted by other people and/or unexpected circumstances. Stinking thinking, if ever there was any. I finally got to a place in my life where I had to cry out to God to help me break the cycles in my life. I prayed and fasted for deliverance from this overpowering mindset. I did not want to treat the symptoms. I needed to get to the root of the issues and be free from the messed-up idea I had of myself.

My journey to healing and freedom highlighted the fact that I despised myself. I also had an issue with procrastination! My procrastination fed my need to be under pressure to complete the task before me, and kept me from managing my time, completing my work on time and/or living my life in manageable segments. By nature, I am competitive and want to be the best at whatever I do, and/or do whatever I do well. This concept in and of itself is not wrong or bad. However, it was my mindset and the motivation behind most of my actions that made it unhealthy and ungodly. My mindset set me up for failure more times than I care to remember. Each time I failed, I blamed myself and said I should not have undertaken it! I beat that pathetic self-defeatist drum over and over again. I could have been the poster child for having a successful pity party.

When I cried out to God for deliverance, I told Him I did not want this stinking thinking in my life anymore. Many times, during my spiritual journey, I was delivered from strongholds, but I still needed to do more to work out my soul's salvation. And although God delivered me from the fear, guilt, and shame that fed my mental dis-ease, I revisited the places in my life where change had occurred and where God had given me new strategies to overcome mental dis-ease. My believing the lies I told myself held me hostage. They hindered me, instead of enabling me to grow into the woman God created and purposed me to be. I learned how to get my daily vitamins from the word of God and put on my daily covering in prayer.

However, the fasting and praying for the revelation of the root cause of my mental dis-ease and the problems it bought into my life were needed so badly that I intentionally set a time and sought God. During the process of prayer, He showed me how my mother and my pastor/uncle were the two people from my childhood, I had put so much trust and value in. What they thought of me influenced my life through their words. Of course, my mother had me in her care the longest, but that relationship was strictly authoritative, and we did not talk. I received orders and did them, or I suffered the consequences. Without thinking, I learned to obey, follow the rules to be rewarded, and it soon became my pattern. Again, I know my mother loves me, she was only capable of showing it in how she took care of and provided for me. There were rare accolades for anything and almost a bewilderment when I advanced in anything, because it was unfamiliar territory for her, and she did not have an opinion about things she had not experienced in her upbringing.

Her actions made me think everyone had the same experiences I did; that is until I was exposed to experiences, she could not relate to. When my mother could not help me with my homework, she prayed for God to open my understanding and give me the ability to do my schoolwork because she had not finished high school before moving from Mississippi. Though she did not have books smarts, she was highly gifted in common sense and trusting God to guide her as she raised my brother and me. Especially when my stepdad was absent from our home because he was incarcerated multiple times. I am happy to say there came a time when he changed his life and became focused on raising his family.

Earlier, I spoke about how I trusted and respected my mother and my pastor/uncle, and how they influenced my life with their words, whether negatively or positively. Which is why I interpret my mother's sparse affection and praise as rejection, and why I rejected my Pastor as a father figure in my life. One Sunday morning during service, his actions, behavior, and words cut me to the very core of my being when he humiliated me in front of the entire Church. Somehow, I developed a vulnerability to their words from their familial roles and connection to me. I allowed their critical words to form my thinking and justified their negative or hurtful actions in my life. After internalizing their words and actions, I determined something must be wrong with me. I commenced to adding that to my mental dis-ease, which led to my belief that I could not go after my dreams and/or goals until I had their approval. This cycle of thinking had me trapped. It was like I was in a house of mirrors, and everywhere I turned I heard their words, but I only saw me, distorted, ugly and unlovable. As crazy as it sounds, I loved them and had an ungodly fear of them, which kept me from telling them about their contribution to the mental dis-ease I dealt with.

I would always sell myself short, I doubted myself, I could not visualize myself beyond the many faults and failures of my past. I could not appreciate what other people saw in me, and I struggled to see myself as God envisioned me, because I felt I had to do something for Him to love me. It was only when I did something for others that I was shown affection. I had interjected these same ideologies into my relationship with God, and limited His influence and guidance in my life, but He would always draw me in through prayer and fasting. I love serving, helping, and encouraging people. Whenever I did those things, they were out of a heart of love. I believed this is all my mother and pastor expected of me, and nothing more. I had put myself in a box that limited me to only look at their hurtful words, actions, and behaviors, and interpret it as my life had no meaning if I was not serving others. In some way, I expected it would redeem me or I would find my worth and value amid the negativity I had welcomed into my life, heart, and mind. I allowed them to define me to the point where I doubted my talents, skills, and gifts unless they were used in Christian ministry! I felt my desire to learn in some way highlighted my mother's limited education, and it was regarded as me trying to show her up or disrespect her. That was the farthest thing from my mind, however, it was the story I told myself, and is why I never openly shared that part of my life. I kept it hidden out of fear of more rejection! When I stepped outside the limitations, I had placed upon myself and started my first business, I was so proud of myself. When I shared it with the people closest to me, I heard comments like, *"You're the one with a college degree, why don't you know how to do this or that…?"*

If my family were proud of me and/or excited for me, I could not hear or see it because my mental and emotional dis-ease only heard the negativity and the words that made me feel worthless and useless. The words had me questioning my ability to run my business. The business God had instructed me to start. This justified the reason I did not go around my mother because I only heard toxic words from her. I cannot honestly say everything she said was negative and/or toxic, but that I had conditioned myself to only hear the negative and toxic words from her. Even if she said something encouraging and uplifting, I did not hear them. I heard the opposite due to the place I was in mentally and emotionally. I had childhood trauma that had never been dealt with, only internalized, which created my belief that something must be wrong with me.

Although I never raised my voice, cursed or was disrespectful to my mother, there were days when I felt her imposing presence that made me feel like I was truly in an emotional, mental, and verbal fight when I left her presence. I did not know how to verbalize my feelings to her, so I did not say anything. I left feeling even more dejected, defeated, and rejected than before I came to see her. While trying to remember when all this started, I remembered when I was fourteen and told my mother I was pregnant. I interpreted her response as negative and was the excuse I needed to doubt everything about myself. I did not feel like I had my mother's acceptance, support, or approval. Sometimes I wonder if my need to serve others was because I only felt like I had my mother's and my Pastor's approval when I did acts of service. Man, that was a heavy weight to carry on top of being fourteen and pregnant.

I now know how much power I had given these two people in my mind that adversely affected and impacted my life. God designed me on purpose and for a purpose! He gave me my mind, talents, and gifts! He knows what He put in me, but the seeds of rejection and low self-esteem, low self-worth were the tools the enemy used through these two people that packed an even greater punch, and caused me to disregard what and who God says I am. What I have learned is I gave them far more control over my life than I realized! As I reflected on this revelation, I am baffled why I am still trying to receive some type of approval from them. Crazy right? I know! This was my reality, and every now and again I feel the pull of my old man trying to pull me back into the insanity that was my life. God was and is still challenging me to recognize, repent, and forgive myself for devaluing the me He made me to be. When I returned back to college after many years, I was married with four children. I had responsibilities for both my home and my job. I felt I had to get the degree to prove something to myself. It was a way to break down the walls I had built to protect myself. The bondage I existed in from the emotional and mental dis-ease I allowed to dictate my life. However, during times of fasting and prayer, the veil was removed, and I discerned the spiritual root of the dis-ease and self-sabotaging cycle I had hid within.

My first college degree was a Bachelor of Science in Chemistry, and I graduated Magna Cum Laude. God then opened another door, and I graduated with a Master of Science in Business Administration a year later. My heart's desire was to help children and adults in the sciences. I wanted to accomplish both in my business and in service to the Church by providing crucial financial bookkeeping. I helped, but never on the scale I would have liked, because I did not want to challenge myself to step into unchartered and unfamiliar territory. Once again, I entered the box because I was afraid of failing if I stepped outside my comfort zone. Not to get too far off track, I realized the moment I released my emotional and mental dis-ease to God for healing, and to truly understand why I thought the way I did, He showed me, me! Acknowledging, recognizing, accepting, understanding, and realizing what I did to myself hurt! We can think ourselves into destructive moments. Once God showed me, myself, I could not deny it as my truth. More than anything I knew I needed to be delivered from myself, the curse of the words I allowed to define me, and my self-sabotaging actions I believed were keeping me safe, but in reality, were holding me back from reaching my greatest potential.

There was never a question for God regarding what He put in me. The issue was me believing in what He put in me. I had allowed the judgments and words of people to cause me not to fully grasp and believe God's word and what Jesus desired to do with and in my life. I needed to release the deep hurts, the repressed anger, and suppressed emotions from years of emotional and mental abuse to God. I had to relive those experiences to remove their paralyzing words that cut deep and hindered me from speaking my truth. For me, it was more hurtful due to who the people were and how long they had been impacting my life in this way. I never expressed my regrets with others or shared with people how I felt because I was afraid, they would judge me, or they too would have something negative to say. So, I did what I had learned to do, I kept it all bottled up inside. This was all based on an event that happened in my life when I was a child. I remember being nine years old when I heard my mother tell my aunt something I had told her in confidence. From that moment on, I did not trust my mother to keep my secrets, and I did not tell her anything else that I wanted to be kept confidential. All this set the tone for the relationship I would have with her throughout my childhood. I lacked the connection that many mothers and daughters have, and it caused me not to trust females in general because I expected at some point, they would betray me.

Free will is exactly that God did not make me change. But the moment I said I love Him, He clearly stated I would keep His commandments. So, my words of love had to match my actions of love, and that required me to change and align with the God of love and be one of many lights of love in the earth. Sometimes, I still struggle with control, pride, and self-centeredness, but I am thankful my Heavenly Father does not allow me to stay in my struggles but corrects me. I repent and align much quicker through my processing in the cocoon stage of my life journey. You can grow through your hardships, pain, mental anguish, because God has given you breath in your body to do so. I know because I grew. My time in the cocoon led to me being healed, delivered, freed from strongholds, and experiencing God as my teacher. When I wanted to quit, I was reminded my life is not my own, and I have been bought with a high price. Therefore, it did no good to fight against God, for my arms were too short. But it made perfect sense to love, obey, worship and praise God as He transformed me from the inside out. Then I could share in my living hope. Through each deficit of my life, God built my character for glorifying Him through it all. Just like the butterfly's process of life is set to go from an egg to an adult; so is the human life set to go from an egg to an adult. Each stage of change is being influenced by either Godly or evil things, we determine by what we feed ourselves during our transformation. What we use at different points in our lives matter. As I got to know me, I was willing to do whatever it took to be transformed by Jesus and become who He created and purposed me to be.

Earlier, I alluded to the humiliation I experienced from my Pastor's words, actions, and behavior. Listen in as I share that story! When I became pregnant at fourteen, my uncle, who is also my pastor, shamed me in front of the whole Church. I think it scared me more than it hurt me! My Pastor, the Man of God, who was commissioned with caring for my soul, called me up to stand in front of the congregation and said because I had sinned, I could not sing in the choir nor participate in any ministry auxiliaries within the Church until after the birth of my child. The church service was packed that Sunday when he sat me down vividly, openly, and horrifically. He did not do it in private to protect me from any embarrassment I may experience. No, he used me as an example, and when he did it publicly, he damaged my self-image, destroyed my self-esteem, and left me emotionally, mentally, and spiritually bleeding on the floor, wishing it would open up and I would fall through. I would rather die than face the stares and gossip of the congregation in the days that followed. How it was done was so devastating that all the people alive today still remember it. The enemy of my soul wanted to take me out before I got to this day, and this age with the psychological warfare I constantly dealt with. The experience sent me down a lonely road, which had me seriously considering suicide. I just wanted the pain to stop. For me to change my focal point, God had me think about the life of my innocent, unborn child. She had a right to live and experience life.

After that service, two mothers of the Church called me over, and hugged me with all the love and support they could give in a hug. Their hugs gave me life because in the span of a few minutes, my entire world had come crashing down. They were angels sent from God and did not know how their actions had saved my life! During the rest of the service, I sat there thinking of ways I could kill myself to make the embarrassment stop. I heard the whispers coming from several members, but only those two ladies spoke to me that day. As I looked at my mother, I saw in her facial expressions she wanted to console me, but she did not reach out or say anything. From that point forward, I rejected my Pastor/Uncle as a father figure and only identified him as the man who deeply hurt and humiliated me. I learned what self-hatred was that day, in the Church, while I was openly humiliated. I attempted to tell myself that he was only doing what God wanted Him to do to show me how great my sin was. But each time I tried to believe that I was reminded if he had genuinely loved me, he would not have done that publicly first. More than being my pastor, he was my uncle. Sometime later, I believed I must have deserved that to happen to me in the way it happened. All I know is I never wanted or desired to experience another humiliating day like that again.

The mass exodus from our congregation happened when other teenage girls got pregnant, who were members of the Church, and left because they did not want to be humiliated the way I had been. What took the cake and sealed the deal of my distrust and rejection of him as a father figure and authority figure in my life was when his daughter and my cousin got pregnant a few years later while unmarried, and absolutely nothing was said to her in the Church like it was said to me. While struggling to come to terms with the hurt I still felt, I could not understand why he singled me out, but not her or others. I began to think I must be the worst kind of human being, because I was not treated in the same way as the Pastor's daughter! I cannot clearly express the magnitude of emotions I experienced! I realize I had repressed some strong feelings from that event, but for me to release them, I had to relive that day again. God knew my desire for freedom was greater than the fear of the emotional pain I would have to feel again. When I was publicly shamed in the Church, I began to have conflicting feelings about the Church. I had been taught to love and forgive in the same building, and by the same person who stripped me of my dignity and humiliated me publicly. At a time when I needed to feel loved, I was ostracized and devastated to the point where I questioned if God hated me!

The event caused me to promise myself if I knew of a young lady who was a pregnant teenager, I would love them through their pregnancy, help them find their way as a new mother, and show the love of God as I taught them to repent of their sin and be restored in God. As God began my healing process, I cried for the teenage girl who was humiliated and mistreated. I moaned for the teenage girl who needed her mother's love and hugs and never received them. I searched my heart for the forgiveness I needed to give my teenage self, so she could release the hurt, pain, and disillusionment she felt. There were times when I cried until I did not have any more tears to cry. What I did not know then, but I know now is every tear I cried Jesus felt and replaced them with the peace I needed to move forward in life. During my fast, I released my fifteen-year-old self safely and securely into Jesus' healing arms. I know that I had what I needed to release the moment. At that point, I lost who I was and became the person I was intended to be – a child of God. In the blink of an eye, God had removed the hurt, pain and confusion and replaced it with the knowledge that He loves me. He loved me so much that He had His Son die just to have a relationship with me. Although, I would not wish any of the embarrassment I experienced on anyone. Not even those who consider themselves my worst enemy. Amid the tears, anguish, hurt, swirling emotions and anger, God showed me during that time of fasting and prayer that I had not forgiven my mother and my Pastor for their treatment of me during crucial moments in my personal development. I thought I had, but God informed me that I had never dealt with the built-up and pent-up emotions that had ushered me into that dark place I had no desire to revisit.

God knew I was ready to do the work it took to be freed from the strongholds that the darkness in my heart and mind had created. My mind became a battlefield between the forces that sought to destroy me and the word of God that I memorized and used daily to live. The enemy of my soul almost had me believing that death was my only option to stop the pain. I begged God to help me find me and break the strongholds that were destroying my life. Sometimes we believe we can handle the spiritual attacks that come our way, or at least I did. There is that stinking thinking again! It was a trick of the enemy, and it pulled me further and further away from God. I was ill-equipped and unprepared to handle the attack I was under. God reminded me that the devil's mission is to kill, steal and destroy. The attack I had ignorantly thought I could fight, and that literally was killing me slowly had stolen my joy, destroyed my self-esteem and self-worth, and attempted to kill me. I felt the hurt so deeply! It felt like the cut had cut so deep that it exposed my bone marrow. I wanted to die, or rather I needed to die to stop the pain. I often think that had I died back then, I would have died in my sin and been separated from God for all eternity. I would not have touched the lives God has assigned me, been able to minister to my own children, and/or shared my testimony of overcoming with those God sends my way. Even though I have never told my full testimony, my compassion, love, and acts of service have introduced many people to the God of my salvation. He literally saved my life and that of my unborn child with a hug. The devices the enemy used was my mind, and the event that happened at the Church. He was instrumental in creating the mental warfare that took place daily in my mind. When I surrendered my will and cried out to God, He taught me how to use the whole armor of God, especially the helmet of salvation and the sword of the Spirit. He taught me to use the sword, which is the word of God, not only to destroy the strongholds in my life, but also to share with others the truth about God being a deliverer, sustainer, and mind regulator.

CHAPTER 4: My Strategies to Overcome and Stay Victorious!

I must give God all the glory, honor, and praise for everything He has brought me through, which has freed me and empowered me to give this testimony of the release moments I have experienced. The enemy's plan not only did not work, but strengthened my faith, my resolve, and my commitment to God's people. My compassion and my heart are for young women, teen moms, young boys, and people who have been isolated, ostracized, humiliated, put through the ringer, and left to die in the filth of hurt, pain, and unforgiveness by the very people who say they are Christians. I learned a lot about God when I was taught by the Holy Spirit, and it is why I am still here to tell this story. Everything the devil meant for evil; God turned it around and used it for my good (Genesis 50:20). The depths of my release are incredible, and when God revealed it to me, I knew I wanted to be freed from darkness. I am here today to tell you that I am free because Jesus Christ died for me and loves me. I am not exaggerating or attempting to demonize anyone! The events I have shared on the pages of this book happened to me! These events made me fight for my mind, my life, and the lives of my children.

The enemy's plan was to use the people in my life to harm me when they should have been there to help me. God, I thank you because deliverance is real, healing and forgiveness are real. My release moments have been tremendous, and the more I release to You, the more You empower me to help others. Because of these release moments, I am who I am today. Glory to God, I am so thankful You kept me, strengthened me, and gave me a voice to speak my truth and be healed. This book is my heart's song! I want everyone to know that if you are in a place of confusion, desperation and hurt at the hands of the people who should have helped you but have harmed you, God has freedom available for you today. Do not give up! The deepest hurt a person feels is no match for God's Love! I am an example of God's unconditional love, and of how He keeps doing the work in me and allows me to be transparent to help others realize their need for Him and cry out to Him. Ages twenty-nine through thirty-five, here's where my cocoon stage began to be tested. In 2002, my high school sweetheart and husband of nine and half years and I divorced It devastated both of us, but it was necessary because we were growing apart instead of growing together, and we stayed civil and friendly to co-parent our children in a loving environment. We had separate homes but kept in communication especially regarding discipline and our involvement in the children's school and social lives. In 2003, one year and two months after the divorce, suddenly and unexpectedly our lives changed forever.

God's Love Overshadows My Stubbornness

March 16, 2003, is a day that will forever be etched in my heart and mind as a day of change, pain, and praise to God! I was thirty-one years old, and it was a Sunday, March 16, 2003. I went to my grandmother's house to help her prepare for Church. As I escorted her to my car to get her situated in the passenger's seat, I heard my cell phone ring. I said to myself that I will answer it in a few moments after I get her in the car. Once she was in the car, I returned the call to my eldest daughter. I called her back thinking maybe she was experiencing pain because she was seven months pregnant. To my surprise and horror, she was crying and saying "*Mama, you have to get to the hospital*!!!! I asked, "*what is wrong?*" She proceeded to tell me she received a call and was told Kendall, my ex-husband, had collapsed at work. They were able to revive him and rushed him to the hospital. They said it did not look good, and I needed to get there. In a panic, I rush my grandmother to Church and told my mother I needed to go to the hospital. From my frenzied movements and the expression on my face, she asked my dad to go to the hospital with me. We left the Church and I drove to the hospital.

We arrived at the Cardiovascular Hospital at Community North, and my dad sat in the lobby while I went to the family room where several family members had gathered. Karen (Kendall's Sister), stepped into the room and said, "*He's gone.*" I asked, "*what do you mean?*" She replied, "*He died!*" I am stunned, and I felt my heart break as I hugged her. While I held and hugged her, she said, "*if you want to go see him, you can.*" I walked down a hallway to the room where his lifeless body laid. There was a tube in his mouth and sheets over his body. I was standing there in disbelief, thinking 'this isn't happening to me, to us!' But it was. It was so surreal that I was frozen in the moment. After I got myself together, I walked around the bed, sat in a chair, and began studying the man with whom I had married, divorced, and still loved. I sat in the chair and shed tears as I called on Jesus! I just could not believe he was dead. The nurse asked if I wanted to call anyone else to come in to see him before they moved his body. I said yes. I wanted my daughters to see him before they moved him.

He was my high school sweetheart and the love of my life! We had three children together, and he accepted my eldest daughter and raised her. We had been through so many ups and downs. Neither of us could blame the other because the failure of our marriage was both of our faults. Deep down, we loved each other and would do for each other, no matter what. Although we were divorced eighteen months earlier, we still had a wonderful friendship. We stayed civil for our children because we loved them enough to put aside the foolishness and put them first. He was the one who took our daughter to her pre-natal appointments because I was not available due to work. This is all unreal! Just the day before, his whole family came together to give his mother a surprise birthday party, and now this.

It was his weekend to have our children. That Sunday morning, they saw him off to work, not knowing that he would never come home again. I notified my family what had happened, my cousin agreed to bring the girls, and my mother kept our son. Our girls were Daddy's girls, he was their handsome superhero! I prayed and asked God for strength in that moment because I knew it was going to be a traumatic and emotional experience for them. As much as I wanted to take their pain away and dry their tears, I could not. When they arrived and saw their father's lifeless body lying on the bed, they cried! I held my babies and cried with them. When they first entered the room, they screamed, "*...Daddy no!!!!! Daddy, get up, we have so much stuff to do. Daddy!!! Daddy!!!*" Every word broke my heart even more. I pulled them close and held them with all my might. I could not stop this moment or change it. We all would have to live through this and learn how to live without him. At that moment, I did not know how to make it through the next eighteen seconds, because this type of hurt cuts in ways and in places not observed with the naked eye.

As a family, we had just stepped into unknown territory. This was our first-time experiencing the death of a loved one, and it floored us. One day he and the children were at his mother's birthday celebration, and the next day he is with the Lord. Now, I needed to help his sister plan his home-going celebration. He had asked some months before during a random conversation, if he died before me, would I sing at his funeral, and I said yes, and asked him what he wanted me to sing. The day of His service, in front of a packed church, I sang as promised. I prayed and asked God to help me honor his request. After the service, we went to the gravesite. His job and co-workers blessed me and the children with an offering they had collected. They expressed their heartfelt condolences and told us he was an outstanding worker who loved his children. I am forever grateful to them for their many acts of kindness.

Now we had to live after the service. I was missing my friend. Even though we had divorced, I thought we would eventually reconcile and remarry. As I grieved, I began to regret our foolish and petty arguments. I had the should haves, could haves, and would haves bad! I found myself traveling down memory lane when the memory popped up of how whenever we had a minor disagreement, I always apologized first. But the last time this happened, I was being stubborn and disobedient to the Holy Spirit's prompting to ask for forgiveness and squash the whole thing. In my stubbornness, I said no, he will come to me first this time. This went on for two weeks. Then I get the call and he is gone forever. I felt so much guilt and condemnation because I will never be able to make amends with him.

I knew I could not stay stuck grieving and feeling guilty. I have four children to raise! I have to be strong for them! Especially since their father is gone. No matter how old they get, they will always be my babies, and this world WILL NOT devour them. I found myself trying to console four children, three girls and one boy, with unique personalities and viewpoints who were grieving in four distinctly different ways. While also expressing their grief differently. My eldest daughter was struggling. She was pregnant, in school, and trying to be strong for her younger siblings while trying to keep it all together, which became even more challenging with each passing day. One day as I thought about it all and realized I am about to become a grandmother and I immediately thought about Kendall and said to myself '*he would have been an excellent grandfather!*' The tears started and the regret tried to take hold again, but no matter how hard it got, God kept giving us strategies (...to talk honestly with each other, to forgive quickly, repent and strengthen each other in the painful moments). I had to make it all make sense as we learned how to live our daily lives without my friend and their father.

My second born, the middle girl, and Kendall's first biological daughter, April, was a Daddy's girl through and through! She was crushed and became rebellious as she sought ways to express the pain she felt while grieving. In her mind, I was the reason her daddy was no longer here. If I had not divorced him and changed everything about our family, he would still be alive! I became the villain in the story she told herself. It hurt me deeply, even though I understood it for what it was, grief. I tolerated her behavior for about a month, but then we had a *come to Jesus* moment. I searched the Bible and asked God to help me help my children. I did not know about the levels of grief or the mental and emotional distress it causes. I did not know it scientifically, but I found out about it because we lived it as a family. My third daughter, Kendra, our baby girl was hurt and wanted her Daddy! She missed him terribly. Our son Antonio missed wrestling and playing with his daddy. While attending to their daily and emotional needs, I did not know I needed to take care of me. So, I did what I always do, I kept it moving. I was working full time, maintaining our household, and preparing for the birth of my first grandbaby. I did something I will never advise any parent to do. I never cried in front of our children nor allowed them to see me grieve.

For whatever reason I thought by crying in front of them, I would show them weakness. I kept telling myself, I had to be strong. During the day, I would be the strong mother who consoled her children, but at night I would cry out to God and plead with Him to help me! I was lost in the hurt and overwhelmed with the memories of our love, our disagreements, our divorce, and our children. The heartache I experienced was a physical pain that got worse with each memory, and even when I did cry, it did not ease the pain. I still loved that man; I just could not believe he was dead. There were many nights when I would cry while singing, Amazing Grace and Precious Lord, solely to fall asleep. Two months after Kendall's death, I graduated from college! Then two and a half weeks later, my granddaughter was born on May 22, 2003, healthy and beautiful! I remember my mother telling me that Beth was having a girl, and I would ask how she knew that. She responded that the old folks down south would say, *"if a man dies, a girl is born, and vice versa."* Although I do not believe in superstition, I have to admit I have noticed the correlation to that saying within my own family. I also know God has the last word on who will be born!

I had been brought to my knees after I came out of my spiritual and mental cocoon. A year later, my maternal grandmother passed that knocked the wind out of me. She had been supportive prayer warrior for me. In my adult years, she was a source of wisdom. Now she's gone! She went home to be with the Lord. Emotionally, this was all new because I had not experienced or understood grief or its process. The heart pain I was experiencing almost led me to commit suicide to get away from the pain and heartache.

Listen, I know the truth of my entire story, and God has taken a detestable, unworthy human to love. He loved me by forgiving me when I repented, teaching me His Word, empowering me with His spirit, and giving me hope to live when I imagined it was easier to die. I know my sins, wretchedness, and how God changed me. That is why I am so thankful for salvation because we all had to be saved from something, sin, emotions, heartbreak and/or heartache to live for God. I learned that spiritual attachments were formed through the sins of my parents and others in my family. I had to renounce and change by God's power, so that those patterns would not be repeated in my children, and as I grew, I prayed for my grandchildren. I am not perfect, but the God in me is wonderful. I experienced mental warfare for most of my life. No, I was not on medications or diagnosed by doctors, but the Great Physician Jesus has and continues to do mighty mental and physical transformations so that I can be a voice of righteousness and holiness for others. Not that I am perfect. I am, however, real, transparent, and know God's love enables me to extend a helping hand to others like it was extended to me.

I know that healing and deliverance are real because it is a part of my story. As I am writing this book, I pray my story will be an encouragement for others to stand on and be empowered as they continue to live and declare the works of the Lord in their own lives. I learned the importance of forgiveness! It started with me forgiving my stepfather, but it did not end there. Over the past fifteen years, I have learned how to forgive my parents, my pastors, my children, my husband, and most of all myself. God has strengthened through the imitate relationship we share. It was developed during the deep spiritual work He has, is and will continue to complete in me that inspires me to share my testimony, character, patience, and love with everyone He allows me to minister to whether in word or deed.

Every trial and situation I have been through was not for me, but for someone else. God is building me into a vessel who will obey Him, and no matter how much I do not understand the whys behind my experiences, He used them to be a beacon of light for those experiencing darkness. I am not extraordinary, but the powerful God in me surely is. I am not the only one who has this testimony, but in order for my children, grandchildren, and future great-grandchildren to know the power of releasing your life into the capable hands of God will yield a reward out of this world. Yes, life has many ups and downs, hurts, and pains, but it also has many joys, triumphs, victories, and a hope that does not disappoint. God is real, and the enemy of our soul is real. By trusting, loving, and growing in God, I realized this world offers nothing in comparison. I had to love the people I thought were unlovable, because I got the revelation that

God loves the unlovable. I had to be patient with my own children because my heavenly father continues to be patient with me. I had to learn to pray for others because someone is praying for me. I learned to trust God and use wisdom when trusting people as I continue to be empowered to live in this world and bring God glory above all else. I had to stand on my Christian faith, learn the hidden tenets of word of God, believe God's word, use it properly, and love people to live in godly wisdom and counsel.

Each release moment pulled out something negative, ungodly, unloving, and shameful and replaced it with God's Word, lessons learned, and a bright future. Just like the stages of the butterfly have to happen, a born-again believer must go through their stages of growth through discipleship. Helping others come through the difficult moments with the truth, and then being willing to move with them as they advance through their process and transformation is empowering.

We are still living and adapting to the new norm. In September 2003, I was approved to purchase my first home. I am still working, providing for my family, supporting our children through their grief, and I am existing, but not living. I was seeing some evidence of my children's healing, but because I made them my focus, I fell into despair. I had neglected to give myself permission to grieve, and I was hurting. It all came crashing down in December 2003. About a week or two before Christmas, I was at my wits end. I could not wear the 'strong woman's mask' any longer that portrayed to the world that I am okay because I was not!!!! I had been strong for everyone else, but I felt like I had no one I could turn to, but God! I did not have anyone to help me! I was in a place in life I never thought I would be in again. I wanted to end my life to stop the pain I had pushed down and closed myself off from Kendall's death. God showed up right on time, just like He did the last time. I was trapped in my mind with the pain from the grief I never gave myself permission to work through. I did not know how to process the regrets, my self-doubts, and the pressures of raising children. I was STUCK!

I reached out to two cousins who saved my life that day. We met up, and within minutes of us talking, the tears started flowing. I shared with them how I felt, my thoughts of suicide and the unrelenting pain I was experiencing. I remember telling them, *"I can't take this pain any longer!"* The more I cried, the more they hugged me! At first, I saw the shock on their faces because 'She is the strong one.' She is the one everyone goes to for help when they need to keep it together. Here I am falling apart, ready to kill myself because I cannot take the pain anymore. That pain forced me to ask for help, and their hugs saved my life. I thank God once again because a hug literally saved my life.

I am going to park here for just a moment to minister to whoever is reading this! I do not care who you are, even if you are strong spiritually, mentally, emotionally, and/or physically. There will come a time in life when your strength will be exhausted, and you will need others to hold you up when you are weak. As I write this, with tears falling, I am reminded how God ordained that day to happen exactly how it happened. He refused to let me die that day. I had my will and insurance policies in a place where my children could find them. They identified how I wanted my children to be taken care of. I was being selfish, I made it all about me because I was hurting. I did not have the strength to think about my children, nor the devastation it would bring into their lives if I committed suicide. I would be putting a huge responsibility on my daughter, Beth, and the rest of my family. I did not have the capacity to think, only to feel. Feel the pain pulling me daily into the abyss of darkness that promised to take away my pain. I kept hearing, day after day, *'If I go into the darkness and end it, you will be free.'* But that is NOT the end of my story! God said, *"Not so!"* God allowed my cousins to be in the right place, at the right time, to answer their phones, and turn an event that would have devastated my children into a new determination to live in and by the power of GOD.

On March 16, 2003, my children were ages fifteen, thirteen, twelve and nine and six months later they were sixteen with a five-month-old granddaughter, fourteen, twelve, and ten, and I am the thirty-two-year-old mother and grandmother. And here I am ready to end it all because my pain (from a scale of one to ten) was on a thousand and it had me STUCK, broken and distraught. I was spiritually under attack and did not know it. But God did, and He broke that spirit off me! Earlier I mentioned, I could not see the past eighteen seconds because of the pain, heartache, grief and regret I was experiencing. By God's grace, it has been eighteen years since Kendall went home to be with the Lord, and our eldest granddaughter is about to graduate high school. He never got to see her or meet her, but I recognize him daily in her. I think about the blessing of grandchildren that exist because of him. I know you may ask, why did I point out our ages because I have eighteen years of testimonies of how God has kept both me and my family through some of our most painful and hurtful days, nights, and everything in between. The scripture that comes to mind is Psalm 30:5, *"For His anger endureth but a moment; in His favor is life: weeping may endure for a night, but joy cometh in the morning."*

Now we are in 2021, and our children are ages thirty-four, thirty-one, twenty-nine and twenty-eight, respectfully. To God be the glory! Everyone has graduated high school and achieved their desired higher educational and/or professional goals and dreams. At one point, all my daughters were married, and my son walked them each down the aisle in memory of their father. I now have ten grandchildren, and I owe it all to God. The mentioning of our children's ages is significant because Kendall was twenty-eight years old when he passed, and to date each of our children has made it to that age and/or passed it. Only God could have done that! I met Kendall when he was fifteen, and I never expected he would die thirteen years later. His death left a hole in our hearts, that only God has been able to fill, and a legacy from the impact he had on the lives of everyone who knew and loved him. As I look forward to the next half of my life, I am eternally grateful that God saved my life with a hug! Over the past eighteen years, God has taught me how to be a friend, maintain friendships and know my limitations. I have pressed through some dark days to be at this moment, and to appreciate the priceless blessings that sprung forth from the fruit of my womb.

I may never fully convey to anyone the totality of my life's journey since March 16, 2003, but God knows! This book has given me the opportunity to talk about my four heartbeats, my children. My eldest, Beth, my compassionate fixer, who will help you and try to resolve everyone's issues. It amazes me how Beth has seen me in my different seasons of growth and still loves me. Beth has a quiet strength that calms and motivates simultaneously. I have watched her as a big sister and mother, and I am amazed at the woman she has become. She is truly a slice of awesome sauce given to me by God. My second born, April, my middle daughter, my challenger, who puts everyone in check when necessary. Her creativity comes from a loving soul who recognizes the beauty around her that inspires her to create beautiful things out of nothing. Even in the rebellious teen years, she challenged me to be better because she is truly a reflection of me. Her protective shell hides a loving and generous heart. I thank God that although we have had time apart to grow into who we are created to be, I am forever grateful that God has created a mother-daughter bond in us that will last throughout the ages. Then there is my baby girl, Kendra, my precious princess! She may be prissy and delicate, but she knows how to turn any situation into an opportunity for her to shine. Although I went through an appendectomy, pneumonia, a collapsed lung, and a cesarean section during this pregnancy, I am reminded every time I see her that God had His hands on her life then, and even more so now. What did not kill her has definitely made her stronger. She was recently licensed as a Minister of the Gospel. My last-born and only son, the outspoken one who believes his words will be heard no matter what. I can lovingly say he makes me honored daily to be his mother. He has a heart for at risk youth to reach them before they get into the legal system. I pray God will reveal his wife, and that she will appreciate his heart and honor it. Each of these unique personalities grew up to have a bond that blesses my heart. I am honored God chose them to be my children and me to be their mother. I am eternally grateful that God stepped in right in the nick of time to speak life into me. I cannot imagine not being here to observe my wonderful children as adults while raising their own children. Because of Jesus, I now recognize my "…*children are a heritage of the Lord.*" (Psalms 127:3)

I have the courage, determination, and desire to share my release moments because of those four heartbeats I just introduced you to. I was broken attempting to live on willpower and physical strength, but God showed me His way. I needed Him, and I needed to learn of Him and develop a personal relationship with Him for myself. When God broke the spirit that had attached itself to me, it was the catalyst God used to forever change my life. I released wrong thinking, my poor self-image, my low self-esteem, my pride, my belief I could be strong for everybody, my belief I did not need anyone, and my self-defeatist behavior and sabotaging ways. I released my babies and grandbaby to God, and the control I ignorantly believed I had. I released my childhood trauma to God, and the spirit of rejection for the gift of love. I released every breath I have held for the gift of breathing. I released doubt, fear, guilt, shame, and pain, and embraced God's love. I released my pain for forgiveness and to overcome the thing personally designed to destroy me. I released the darkness for the light. I released the pain of suicide for the gift of life.

The events that occurred in 2003 were not ideal, but necessary. God knows each of my days, what they will hold, and how I will get through them, because He created me in His image on purpose and for a purpose. I had to work hard to embrace joy, but when I looked at my grandbaby's face, I was instantly reminded the joy of the Lord is my strength. While releasing the moments I believed defined who I am, I learned to embrace the freedom through the power of God. I learned to accept the liberty God offers to have the freedom to live a life hid in Him. The experiences in my life have helped me not be surprised at the tremendous adversity and/or warfare that comes my way. I look to Jesus, the giver of my strength, and I say, "*I am not new to this, I am true to this!*"

God's grace has shown me I must be true to God first, take care of myself next, and then show up for my loved ones as God dictates. I have learned how to love while allowing God to shine through me, so my family, friends and others can have their own testimony of how God brought them through!

Allow me to explain how reliving this memory of my children's pain helped me this year with the death of my biological father. Well, Lord, only You could orchestrate how I would pour out a painful moment when a life in my family line was transitioning to be with You. Although we knew the day would come, this is another moment to release.

On May 4, 2021, I received a phone call informing me my biological father had passed. There was no guilt or regret, nor was there any sorrow, because two weeks earlier I visited with him and his wife. I know it was a divine moment because his wife, Mrs. L, wanted to share her heart with me. Previously, I shared my brother, and I were the result of an affair my father had with my mother. Here I am, in their home, where they raised their six children born during their marriage, experiencing this man who gave me the other half of my DNA. I am listening as Mrs. L shared how she never interfered with my father, kept him from interacting with my brother and I, or from visiting with us. Mrs. L stated she had forgiven him for his infidelity several years earlier. After listening to her, I asked if he had accepted Jesus Christ as his Lord and Savior, and she said he had. I was grateful for that. It had been over fifteen years since I had last seen my father. Although we did not have a father-daughter relationship, I knew who he was. My brother interacted with him more than I did. When I introduced myself, his eyes lit up? I do not know if he comprehended everything I said during our conversation, from the dementia and cancer diagnoses. He was in hospice at home because his doctors said they could do nothing more for him. They felt it was best for him to be surrounded by his family and loved ones in his final moments.

I prayed before I went to their home and asked God to prepare me for this visit and for the Holy Spirit to give me the words to say to him. When I went to the door, I felt like running away, because I do not remember ever meeting his wife before that day. If I am being honest, the whole thing felt awkward. I was coming face to face, for the first time, with the wife of the man who had an affair with my mother that produced both my brother and I. I was not sure if she would even let me in her home. While I was there, I recognized one of my half-brothers who I had not seen for about ten years. God knew exactly what I needed to experience during my visit with my father and his family. I am forever grateful for the visit, the closure of a relationship I did not fully know, but that I needed, and the peace I experienced when I left was beyond understanding.

On May 4, when I received the call, I was thankful that I had followed God's direction and visited him. Later I called and spoke to Mrs. L to give my condolences to her and their family. I have been praying for the entire family because I know how it feels to lose a loved one. My heart went out to them because I knew the full impact of the loss had not yet hit them. The days to come would be arduous, as they developed a new normal that did not include him. I also prayed for myself for God to help me deal with any feelings that may surface from our visit and his death. I wanted to maintain my peace, and only God can help me with that. I have no hostility in my heart or mind towards him, his wife, or my mother. It is part of my history. A history that teaches me the importance of forgiveness and how to have compassion towards all people no matter who they are or what they have or have not done. I am thankful God knew how I would enter the earth, and that the sins of my parents were not new to Him. Regardless of the circumstances surrounding my conception and birth, I know I was created on purpose because God ordained me to LIVE.

I have a non-traditional family tree. God saw fit to have me born into this family and have this lineage. I do not know what the future holds, but I would like to have some type of relationship with my other siblings. I do not know anything about them, and I would like to communicate regularly with them. I believe God can heal us from anything that may have impacted and/or affected us negatively during our childhood through our open communication with Him. Especially if it has anything to do with my brother and me. Although they knew we existed and knew about our parent's affair, I did not and still do not know them. My mother has always been guarded with that part of her life, and while we were growing up, she only shared his name with us. I have no desire to go back in time to ask the whys or focus on the what ifs. I am focused on moving forward and learning what God's purpose is concerning these matters.

I have felt a lot of shame and embarrassment regarding my parent's affair, and the circumstances around my conception and birth. I allowed the enemy of my soul to make feel me ashamed. As I said earlier, my family is who they are, and I accept them for who they are even if no one else does. God has given me peace, which is priceless during the challenging moments of life. I have chosen not to try and control any of this, but to allow God to do what He does best; allow His will to play out in the lives of His people. Whenever I take my last step and/or last breath, it is my desire for my life to bring God glory. We all have a journey and story of how we came to be, and it was not a mistake or accident in the eyes of God. Well, I just want to thank You, Father God, for another release, and may You be glorified in every part of this release moment.

Just like most people, I take an inventory of my life every time someone I know dies. I do it because I know it could have been me. It could have been my children making home-going arrangements for me! The compassion I want extended to me is the same compassion I extend to others. I can only do that from the work God has already accomplished in my heart. I may not be where God wants me to be, but I am not where I used to be. The various levels of releasing for the different pivotal moments in my life are now making more sense each day I live. Some people never put in the work to tell their unique story, but God has given me this moment as a point of reference for my children and grandchildren to comprehend that their mama or grandma is not perfect, but is perfectly loved by the perfect God she serves. What I thought made me insignificant and unworthy is exactly why God loves me so much. My biological father may not have been part of my life, but my heavenly Father is the conductor of the orchestra of my life even before I was born. Every moment I did not quit is because He strengthened me and gave me the tools to build a life hid in Jesus Christ. One thing that has always amazed me about God is when I went through bankruptcies, a divorce, career rejection, peer rejection, and even Church organizational rejection, He never rejected me! He kept showing me how much He loves me. He reminded me He accepted me in the beloved, and nothing can separate me from His love.

Hallelujah!!! In all honesty, it took me a minute to believe and begin living it to get to today. I never had the desire to quit. He made me a warrior. I must complete this journey called life and do what God purposed me to do. I cannot lay down, roll over and/or be satisfied with mediocrity! I must strive for Godly excellence.

I remember being told, "...*it does not take all that to serve God and enjoy life.*" I would ask in return, "*What makes you think I am not enjoying life?*" It amazes me how people will criticize others from their perception of their life. They are making assumptions without knowing the whole story. Early in my Christian walk, God told me to tell my story, and I immediately replied, no problem. I will tell of Your blessing and the multiple things You have done for me. He said, "*...no tell all of it the good, the bad and the ugly.*" I said, "*I cannot do that!*" He replied, "*...you will do just that.*" I have shared parts of my story at the appropriate times because I had to be mature enough to handle the weight of the assignment. I knew I had to be obedient, even though it made me uncomfortable to tell my truth. Now, I am amazed at how God transformed my mind, freed my spirit, and released me after He did the work in me.

I have heard people describe me as committed, persistent, loyal, wise, and dedicated to name a few. I always pause because I live the Christian lifestyle as directed by the Holy Spirit. I have learned that there are specific things I need to do daily to remain focused on God and become who He has created and purposed me to be. I am not trying to be perfect, but I am pressing towards the mark for the high calling in Christ Jesus, and I am all in. Writing the words and talking about myself has proven to be one of the hardest things I have had to do thus far. There was a time when I would beat myself up and tear myself down while believing that would keep me humble. I have also struggled to accept compliments and/or accolades. That was until I believed God fully in who I am in Him. If I am honest, I still sometimes struggle with accepting compliments and accolades. However, when those times arise, I ask God to help me with my unbelief and transform my mind and thinking. I challenge myself to remember that I am made in the very image of God. I would love to say it gets easier to submit and surrender to the will of God, but more and more these days I am doing it while totally trusting and seeking God's strength. It is only by using God's strength that I can complete this book, attain a master's degree, pursue counseling opportunities, and handle my ministry responsibilities. God is who gets me through each day. In January 2021, I launched my blog, and for the past 11 years, I have been sending out morning encouragement and inspirational texts to people. It is only by the grace of God that I can complete my responsibilities hourly, daily, and weekly.

Rosetta Priestly

CHAPTER 5: Encouragement to Keep Pressing.

God disrupted my sleep and my life until I completed this assignment. An assignment that has helped me release the last vestiges of lingering self-doubt, insecurities, and/or fear. So, I spoke out the essence of my book to myself and recorded these words on the pages of this book. *"Release Moments"* houses the emotions, situations, horrific scarring, emotional damage, mentally impairing, and spiritually confining times I experienced during three or four poignant events that forever changed my life. These events pop out as poignant moments, where I had to come to the end of myself, like the prodigal son, to release them and LIVE.

I had to grow into the person who wanted to, scratch that, needed to change. I had to find the courage to follow through with the actions to recognize the change happening in my life. When I finally realized and accepted that I needed to change, I realized who God had been trying to tell me I am and who He is in my life. People say once you take the first step, all the other steps are uncomplicated. Well, I cannot say that is true. The first release moment I experienced dealt with me being real with who I was, learning not to be concerned with who people believed me to be, and the struggle to believe I am who God said I am. I had to be real about the trauma I experienced and how I was observing the world through the shaded lenses of incorrect thinking, and incorrect spiritual reactions, until I learned through the Holy Spirit and God's word how to know what is right and develop the skills and tools to live my life fully. Learning to accept that God loves me forced me to begin a deeper belief and understanding of His word when He said He will never leave nor forsake me. All of which has built the foundation on which my testimony stands today.

Releasing the events, hurts, pains, and emotions is necessary for you to go through those rough and strenuous times to learn, or even relearn God's way to succeed took commitment and work. Release moments are events and experiences I had that someone else did not survive to talk about. God has brought me on the other side of through to healing and wholeness, and I am a living to tell the whole truth and nothing but the truth.

In 2018, God gave me the word RELEASE to represent the season of transition I was going through, as I learned how to obey God in all things. I learned how to release, relinquish, and give up my whole being to God. Without me knowing it, God was teaching me how to not get caught up in Christianity, the traditions of men, and/or the fear of man (humankind) to ensure I was not returning to the things He was delivering and healing me from. He knew that if things did not change, I would get to a certain point in my life and get stuck. He knew I would not be able to deal with the anger and would be holding unforgiveness in my heart. All of which would hinder my breakthroughs. My reality at the time was that I wanted to stay in the state of being broken because it was familiar. Fighting for deliverance was new and baffling. More than anyone else, I know what happened to me, how it affected me, and frightened me, but that is not where my story ends! God delivered me, and I cannot hold my peace. I must speak my truth for someone else to be inspired, delivered, set free and/or encouraged. As well as be enriched and uplifted with the understanding that everyone has release moments. Some may call it an epiphany or their breakthrough; but for me they are my release moments. I had to obey God and release those moments that I had allowed to define ME!

In the early years of my childhood, the happenings in my life were not of my own making, but were directed and influenced by my parents, grandparents, and other family members. Which caused me to believe if anything went wrong, it was because of me! Now of course, I understand it was a trick and a plot against me meant to get me caught up in that cycle of thinking, feed my low self-esteem, and my poor self-image; and keep me in bondage tied to the opinions, expectations, and thoughts of other people. For me, the cycle began at age seven and lasted until I was about forty-six years old. I had to learn how my body, mind and spirit had been damaged. I had to go into the deep hurts and brokenness for God to heal me. It was when God revealed to me the cord used to keep me tied to the rejection, fear, character assassination, and deception that I understood it all for what it was, a lie. Whether it was due to people, places, and/or things in my mind, I was the reason these things happened to me. I was convinced I caused them and deserved the mistreatment I experienced. Although these were all lies, I believed in them during the early formative years of my youth and the roots run deep. I had to expose them and the power they had over my life to have the freedom God promised in His word (*"Now the Lord is that Spirit: and where the Spirit of the Lord is, there is liberty..."* –2 Corinthians 3:17).

As a child, I developed the mindset of being responsible, which taught me what I needed to do to please my mother. This training governed my life because I believed everyone was raised like me. Surely all children knew how to wash clothes by hand, mop, wash dishes and cook certain foods. They knew how to change diapers, feed, and bathe their younger siblings. This was my responsibility while my mother worked. I did not receive praise, allowance and/or perks, it was what was expected of me, period. This was my life, and as a seven-year-old second grader, I was being groomed to be a homemaker and wife. Socializing was not part of my life. I was to assist my mother with the responsibilities in our home. It was ingrained in me at an early age, and like so many others, it did not leave as I got older. It became the foundation where more responsibility was added, on top of more responsibility. Some people wonder why I am who I am; this is the reason. I am structured this way from the lessons I learned early in life.

I learned to live my life with an authority figure who gave me the instructions they expected me to carry out. From parents, family members, teachers, and/or pastors, each person gave me things to do, and I did then because they were authority figures and knew best, right? I believed their words and/or instructions were the gospel truth. I was naive and obeyed them as an authority figure in my life. This structured obedience was how I thought everyone lived. People took advantage of me because they knew I would obey and not ask questions. From that point through my life, that is how I believed my life was to be. Until I received clarity, understanding, and learned that not every authoritative figure will tell you what is right.

Earlier, I mentioned that one of my "Eye Opening" moments was when I realized my mother did not know everything. It was then I learned an essential life lesson: a person can only help you if they have been helped mentally, spiritually, financially, and/or socially. If they have not, they can hinder you or even worse use you. I seemed to be a slow learner in this regard because I learned this lesson time and time again. Later in life, I discovered my dependency on people for guidance and direction was misplaced, and that God needed to be my source for me to receive what I needed. To have access to the liberty, as described in 2 Corinthians 3:17, I had to go beyond anything I had referenced in my life at that point and become exposed to the bare bones, root, unproductive and negative behaviors present in my life. Which forced me to identify who did what to me, when it happened, and how it impacted and affected me. That is when God turned my mistakes and messes into messages for His glory to become blessings to and for someone else.

This is not how I wanted things to happen or progress in my life. Remember, my life was guided and led by forces outside my control, but God! He knew what I did not know and enabled me to keep going wherever He had determined I should go. It amazes me daily how He declared who I would become and the lives I would touch long before I accepted the possibility of being used by God in any way. God redirected me to become a person who positively affected and impacted my children, grandchildren, and other family members, friends, co-workers, and even my community. The path in which my life has taken has granted me the opportunity to touch people in magnificent ways because of the grace and mercy of God. People I would have never guessed would have any significance in my life, but God knew! The release moments that surrounded how I was brought up, how I allowed the authority figures to influence my life, how I regarded myself, and how I interacted with the world around me left me needing to be accepted and approved by people, instead of looking to God to accept, approve and show me my worth. I started allowing the influence of television, music, and my peers to expand my thinking, which sped up my need for release moments long before I ever had the first one. I learned more about God, and the more I learned, the more I wanted to learn. Then one day it dawned on me, I had to release the things I allowed to define and set my life's path toward God to become who I am today.

I pinpointed age seven as the beginning of this structure for authority and responsibility in my life. At age eleven, I experienced a trauma that forever changed my life. Age fourteen and fifteen included the influence of peers and exposed my naivety and my need for the explanation I never received about life. I did not know teenage boys were hormones and war zones and viewed teenage girls as targets. As a young teenage girl in high school, I had crushes on boys, but did not know how to talk to them, let alone interact with them. I believed if you met a boy, they would become your husband, and you would live happily ever after. Boy, is that not even close to the truth! A teenage male told me that he loved me, and I was in love. I learned the difference between authority and submission, but I lacked the knowledge of affection and understanding the consequences of allowing hormones to rule your decisions. I was immature and did not equate that a boy would say or do anything to get what they want from a girl, which was sex. I was young and dumb and believed whatever he said to me because I wanted him to love, accept and approve of me so badly. I craved it because I lacked it in my life. On top of that, I had not been shown what a relationship between a girl and boy was supposed to look like. I made what I saw on TV and in movies scenarios as my plumb line for life. Of course, life was learned the hard way! I learned sex was the motive and not love! It was not ideal to learn that after you have sex for the first time, nor when discovering it can lead to you becoming pregnant. The part that hurts the most is being looked down on for being naive and unknowledgeable about sex, love, and life. I felt dejected and rejected from my lack of knowledge, and no one was willing to teach me what I needed to know.

The humiliation, the whispers, the fear, the hurt, the suicidal ideations, the unforgiveness, and the shame played itself out in my life until I learned the importance of forgiveness and when I began writing this book. I could discern how the hurt, shame, and devastation played a major role in my choices and the consequences I experienced. In all honesty, I struggled with telling you, the reader, how stupid I was for believing a teenage boy who said he loved me. I then asked myself, *"Who wants to tell the world that?"* Then God assured me it is a message that needs to be read and heard, because there are girls making the same choice today and for the same reasons.

I asked God if He wanted me to tell how hurt, insecurity, being traumatized and scarred from pivotal moments impacted my life to other people? The answer was a resounding, *"Yes!"* Once again, I struggled with the task before me, because I was continuously reminded that the people who hurt me were the people who should have helped me. Let me clarify this. I did not want anyone to condone my sin. I did not know how to bear the weight of the effects of my sin. I discovered that the actions or reactions to me becoming a teenage parent were not God approved, nor were the decisions and actions of those in positions of authority. Even though it was hurtful, demoralizing and traumatizing, they did the best with what they had available to them.

The enemy of my soul used key people and their words to damage my spirit and leave scars in my heart and mind. Every word equated to a physical hit or blow to my body. Hit after hit came, especially after everyone found out I was pregnant with child number two. The tone and words being spoken against me became them saying "…*if you did not have sex, you would not have to get talked about*!" Understanding their issue with my second pregnancy was perplexing, especially since I equated sex with love and believed it was how you expressed your love to a person. I knew I loved my high school sweetheart, and he genuinely loved me. I better understand why God instructs us to get married before having sex, because when you do not follow His plan, it leads to a life of difficulty when it does not have to.

I can now appreciate the blessing of meeting my high school sweetheart, eventually falling in love, and getting married. We helped each other through some crazy family issues and learned to grow and love each other in and through the tough times. As we navigated our daily relationship and eventual marriage, I better understood how people will judge you, but never have any desire to learn the why behind your choices and/or behavior. People closest to me examined my current situation and/or lifestyle and made a declaration over my life. The only issue with that behavior is that only God has the final say. I am eternally grateful that my life and where I will spend eternity are not left in the hands of the same people who judged me and found me lacking. I guess for me it was even more hurtful that the people judging me were my family and loved ones, and for whatever reason they felt justified in doing it. Their approval and acceptance of me were important, and I began to internalize their judgment and allowed it to become a destructive force in my life. It negatively affected how I perceived myself and my self-worth. What God has shown me since is this was a lie from the pit of hell, and He showed me I had to be delivered from the guilt, shame, fear, and strongholds created from me internalizing their words to survive.

While growing up, I prioritized the authority figures in my life because if an adult said some things to me, I thought I deserved it, and accepted it as the truth. It played into what the enemy had planned for me. I found myself stuck on the merry-go-round of a negative thinking cycle about myself. I wanted off, but I did not have anyone to stop it from spinning, so I could jump off. The fear of failing, of not being accepted and being regarded as worthless, had me paralyzed in place and unable to move into whatever God had next for my life. The enemy got even bolder when he saw how his actions were impacting my life, and constantly bombarded my mind with negative words and thoughts. According to him, I could not do anything right. Instead of meditating on the word of God, day, and night, I meditated on those negative words and thoughts. During sparse moments of calm, I found myself constantly looking for a way for my family or people to finally accept me. God later revealed to me that the hurtful moments in my life were turned inward and used, as I blamed myself for the things that went wrong or happened, because I believed, as everyone else did, it was all my fault. I just beat them to the punch in communicating it.

God spoke through the Bible and Biblical teachings that I needed deliverance, and the strongholds can only be broken once I forgive the people who had spoken death into and over my life. You know, the people who were supposed to love, care, and protect me because they are my family. While attempting to please my family and people, I realized I had not pleased anyone, not even myself. I was killing myself, trying to please everyone else, or be competent enough to combat the words used to speak death into my life. I believed from fifteen to twenty-three that in some people's eyes I was nothing until they said I was something. As I share this story, I am amazed by the amount of power I gave these people in my life, and I better understand now why I began to believe that suicide was the answer to stopping the emotional and mental pain I experienced. The devil is such a liar. I gave him the power to use guilt, hurt, and shame to manipulate and control me. But God! God woke me up spiritually and broke those spirits off me while teaching me His word and what unconditional love looks like. No one will ever take me back to that place of bondage again. I will no longer give anyone the power to crush me with their words, nor will I allow another person's opinion of me to matter above my own! God accepts me! God created me! No, He did not want me to sin and suffer the consequences of my sins. The awesome part of my story is He forgave me when I repented of my sins! Yes, there were consequences for my sin, but there are also blessings from my obedience. God knew for me to learn the lessons life is to teach me, and to grow spiritually, I needed to be given the information to develop the tools I will put into action to fully understand what God is doing in and with my life.

It hurts me to say this out loud! I was not learning spiritual lessons well because I kept trying to put those lessons in a secular setting or mindset while expecting a Godly result. I wanted people to change, and God expected me to change.

I wanted apologies and acceptance, and God expected me to learn forgiveness and become whole in Him. For me, religion with religious spirits kept me in bondage, B.U.T. (Bowing Under Truth) a relationship with Jesus freed me like nothing else could. God provided a way out in Himself, but I had to have faith to take the leap and believe Him with all of me. It is due to God's grace that I have had, and still have so many victories, and they are all for His glory. My commitment and the fortitude I have to endure when quitting is easier is from Jesus, and honestly, that is why I am still here. I was never part of the armed forces, but I am part of God's army. My children are alive because I warred in the spirit when the enemy attacked them in various seasons of their lives. Life has taught me that people will categorize and criticize you, and few will applaud or appreciate you.

Later in life, I found out my mother and a couple of aunts had children as teenagers with older men. Like me, they naively fell in love with them. However, no one ever told their stories. I cannot say knowing this information would have helped me or not, but I can say, had I known it, I would have processed the information I received differently. I would have been better equipped to understand their viewpoint, because I would have realized they could relate to me and wanted the best for me instead of merely judging me. I fought myself for many years because I thought these things should happen due to my choices. As a Church girl, I experienced the hypocrisy of church folk up close and in person. I believed the negative words of church folk were correct because they were God's elite, and I needed them to get me in line with God. My experiences with them taught me that just because a person can remember, and quote scripture does not mean they live by them. There is a difference between going to the church building and being the Church (Jesus Christ's body of believers) and knowing what the Bible says and doing it. All of it challenged me to learn from the teachings of the Holy Spirit, as I began to recognize that God used what I learned to change me. God showed me that when He called me, He justified me through Jesus. It still amazes me today that He loves me and has never attempted to kill or condemn me. It is His desire that I become a living testimony for someone else. My children were the first to recognize God's change in my life and His forgiveness. What I know for sure is God will forgive us when we recognize our sin, repent, and ask for healing and wholeness. I am thankful to God that I have experienced His forgiveness, healing powers and love.

I had to release the core of my rejection, hurt and pain to God. It was an intense time for me, and although I hate to admit it, I believed God would treat me like some church folk had treated me, and I did not trust Him enough to be vulnerable with Him. A vulnerability that became easier as I learned to trust God more. I avoided hurtful people, places, and situations, even though I was built to fight the forces of evil that sought to destroy my soul. It became clear to me that I could only fight in, though, and with the power of God. It took years for me to fully understand how to use and operate my whole armor and gain the full strength I needed to war in the Spirit. However, when I released everything, I was and was not to God, I began to feel the strength He gives His warriors. I have never regretted my decision to fully lean on, obey and trust God. One of the challenges I had to overcome, and not allow to impact my life nor negatively affect me, is when people bring up what you have done wrong in life, instead of affirming you through the word of God. I now realize God never intended for His children to seek validation from perfectly imperfect people.

He wants our hearts and minds to stay on Him as we learn how to trust and believe Him above all else. The hurt, pain, disappointment, disillusionment, heartache, and unforgiveness I felt back then reminds me daily to be the dispenser of compassion and empathy I wish someone had given me during those pivotal moments in my life. It would have helped me release them so much sooner. Which is why I made the commitment to never make another person feel like I felt when I was at my lowest.

I have a heart for the underdog, because at a point in my life I needed someone to show me the love and compassion I wanted to receive. The love and compassion I finally discovered can only come from God. My release to God meant being transparent and broken before Him. In the beginning, I did not know how it would turn out, but I knew it had to be better than what I had endured so far. It was difficult for me to accept or understand the Christian phrase *"God is good all the time and all the time God is good."* It was not represented in my life because I equated God with the church folk I encountered regularly. Especially since the situations I faced were not pleasing, and I did not see how any good could come from them, but God did.

As a child, I was an early learner, but I did not know how to be social, make friends and/or be one. I was hindered by the limitations of my parents. In my home cooking, cleaning, and sewing were necessary skills, but not in school, college, and/or the workplace. Those skills did not benefit me. Just as I was taught structure in my home, I needed to be taught how to structure my life outside of our home. I did not understand the relationship between a man and woman in a marriage relationship. The only example I had was the marriage I observed between my mother and stepfather. I saw marriage as an escape for me. The escape I needed to get out of my mother's home and from under her rule. I was ready for a change, and I wanted wholeness and understanding on what God wanted from me here on this earth. I needed to understand how I could impact others while impacting my children.

For someone who prided themselves on being intelligent, having to admit I did not know it all and release the insecurity and inadequacy it highlighted to God was challenging. Something I was ashamed of. To feel safe and have a sense of security, I needed control over everything in my life. By having control, I believed I could avoid the pain that found its way into my life. Well, God let me know that I did not and could not control anything in my life. He did. God showed me how to understand and appreciate people. From His guidance and that of the Holy Spirit, I discovered how to be empathetic to and concerned with other people's situations. He began allowing me to learn how to love those I thought were unlovable. I was a quick study because He showed me how much He loves me, even when I did not love Him. (*"But God commendeth his love toward us, in that, while we were yet sinners, Christ died for us."* –Romans 5:8) Although I went to Church, the bulk of my Biblical and Spiritual training was by the Holy Spirit. Wherever there was lack in my life, God used it as an opportunity to teach me and then share what I learned with others. In the same way I went to school to learn about Chemistry and Business Management, God used my life as my classroom, where I was taught Biblical counseling while being counseled by God. This type of on-the-job training was highly effective for me. Simply being told to read and memorize scriptures, as well as being encouraged to pray, did not offer the guidance I needed to counteract the powerful hits and trauma I had experienced that left me struggling to understand God's role in my life and how to build my faith. In the process of me releasing myself to God, He in turn released the knowledge, courage, wisdom, and insight I need to live peaceably in this world.

Everything God taught me was through revelatory learning. It was revealed to me why people believed or acted the way they did. Listen, when you do not know where you have come from, it can show up in unexpected ways, and sometimes it may even come back to bite you. As I previously shared, I was conceived as the result of an affair between my father and mother. Without realizing the truth surrounding my conception and birth, my husband and I both had affairs during our marriage. Affairs that we did not know were part of our family's history. Sometime later during our marriage, we found out that our fathers had affairs. Knowing this only states we were predisposed to have an affair, but it did not have any bearing on the decisions we made during our marriage. We sinned and broke our covenant to each other and suffered for it. I am unaware of our fathers' backstory that led to their affairs. However, for us, we lacked the skills to deal with the emotional hurt we each had suffered during our developmental years. Which resulted in us both hurting each other, and that led to us being responsible for the break-up of our marriage and our home. When that happened, what I thought I knew about my past and serving God went out the window. Immediately thereafter came the guilt, shame, and fear. Fear of the unresolved hurt and unforgiveness that came to light once we divorced. God showed up and exposed me in such a way it humbled me. He showed me, ME, and it was hideous! I can very easily blame everyone else for what I had not been taught about God, faith, and life, but God shut that down immediately. He loved me through the ugliness that was me and showed me how to take the lessons I had learned (the good, the bad, and the ugly) to tell my testimony of how I overcame, built a loving relationship with God, and faced the demonic forces that sought to take my life. Every time I share my testimony, there is at least one person who is thankful that I shared my truth with them.

In everything, I have shared thus far, one thing has not changed, when a person is ready to surrender ALL to God, they are at the moment of release. Surrender may start the process, but faith finishes it! My process began with me wanting to be free of the guilt, shame, fear, bitterness, anger, rejection by others and rejection of myself! I wanted to stop going to Church service and leaving the same way or worse than when I came. I wanted to experience God and have an encounter with Him that provided me with the roadmap to escape the bondage my life had me drowning in. Growing up in Church affords you an insight that people who are not raised in Church do not have. I had learned how to say all the right things, at the right time, to keep people from digging into my private life. Deep in my heart, I knew there was more to God than Church services, auxiliaries, and singing in the choir, and more than anything else I wanted whatever it was in my life.

When I tell you that God is the master strategist, take me at my word. It was so strategic how God orchestrated moments in my life through my jobs, academics, and even books to give me the answers and examples of how to live for Him. God showed me how to structure my household, how to be a wife, and how to be a mother to our children. When I look back on my life, I am amazed at the many preconceived notions and wrong thought processes I had. God gave me a crash course in living righteously in the way

He determined it should be. I remember somewhere during the process; I stubbornly believed my way was better than God's way. God spanked me for many days until I did it His way. Being the hard-headed Christian I am, I gave up and gave in after realizing I was fighting a losing battle. The experience taught me, more than anything else, the importance of being inside the will of God, believing His word, and being obedient. He loved me enough to correct me, redirect me, accept me, and show me my purpose, because He determined I was needed in the kingdom for such a time as this. He continued working in and with my life because He would not leave me in the state of sin and carnality, I had lived in.

Some choices and decisions I made are astounding to me today. Like when I experienced the death of Kendall, my ex-husband, my best friend, and the love of my life. The grief I experienced and my belief that I needed to act strong for my children nearly killed me. Had I not had the presence of mind to reach out for help, I would not be here today telling this story, but God! That experience and the emotional and mental abuse I put myself through brought me spiritually to the end of myself, and I had only one option; to look up and draw from God. For some reason, I have an odd connection with experiencing tragedy while in school. Just when I was about to graduate with my bachelor's degree, I lost Kendall, and then in 2004, my grandmother passed away when I began school to attain a master's degree. In both cases, I am in school struggling and broken from the devastation I felt at losing two of the most important people in my life. Losing my grandmother so soon after Kendal hurt in ways I cannot describe. She taught me so much, and to honor her memory, I worked hard to stay focused on supporting my family and completing my degree. In June, 2012, when I became an empty nester and wondered what to do with myself, God told me to go back to school for Biblical Counseling. Then in October 2012, my stepfather unexpectedly passed away, and in November 2012, my children's other grandfather (my former father-in-law) passed. Once again, I am struggling under the weight of two losses so close together. They were crushing both me and my children emotionally. To deal with the grief, and take care of my children and myself, I took a month off from school to gather myself before returning to complete my degree.

I do not know what else can possibly happen in this year, 2021, but so far, my biological father passed away, and one of my granddaughters tried to commit suicide in the same week. The one constant in every instance has been God's ability to help me stay focused while trusting Him to provide for my every need. As I think about my educational career, I am reminded of the story my aunt talked about the time I went into labor with one of my children while preparing for a test I had to take. In my life, there has been something about the structure of staying focused in the face of adversity, trials and/or issues while completing a task that drives me. The same has been true with completing this book! For the past several weeks, I have had to fight daily with some type of distraction or hinderance. This evening, hours before the deadline I set, I was called to defuse a situation that stopped me from typing. It has literally been one thing after another. As with everything else in my life, I am putting this book, whoever it reaches, and its assignment into the capable hands of God. Because of you, the reader, I am thankful God would not allow me to quit, even when it was the most convenient thing to do. While writing this book, my heart and mindset changed from this being an assignment by God to another moment God used for me to release those things in my life never meant to be carried with me into my next season of life. It is this simple for me, if the many deaths I have experienced while in school did not stop me, I cannot allow anything to stop me while I complete what God has given me to do.

It would be easy to blame others for the wrong I have experienced in my life, but I have to take ownership of my mess-ups and mistakes, heartbreaks, and heartaches, and release them to God through forgiveness (for everyone involved and for myself) to be healed and/or delivered. Relinquishing my perceived control to God is not easy. As a matter of fact, it hurts in the beginning. I am writing my life's journey and putting it on display for every person who says I am so strong! They need to understand it was God who has shown me what real strength looks like and pulled the fortitude out of me from the strength I received from Him to fight for my life and the lives of my children. I could have easily given up and died at that moment. People say Rosetta, you are so wise! And I would think, 'am I?' Wisdom comes from experience and learning the lessons life teaches you. My wisdom comes from all that God has brought me through, the lessons I have learned, and the obedience I have to God's direction and instructions. With that being said, I am quick to tell everyone to obey God, prevent chastisement, and bask in the blessings of God. Someone once told me that I am smart. I wondered, 'am I?' I made the choice submit to God and live for and in His purpose. I never imagined my life would have such an impact on so many lives. I truly desire to keep having release moments because every time I do it will bless me and others, and for that I am thankful. If I did not make it clear, please hear me when I say the Church (Christ's body of believers) did not hurt me, but certain people in the local Church's congregation did. God showed me the difference while teaching me how to forgive them and live.

Once I started maturing in my faith and relationship with God, the religious things I had been taught from the traditions of man no longer satisfied me, and I desired to go deeper. While going deeper in prayer, studying the scriptures, and building a more intimate relationship with God, I began to understand He was preparing me to release my will, recognize myself as the sinful person I am, and seek God for repentance, forgiveness, deliverance, healing, and wholeness, which all led to me experiencing additional release moments initially hidden even to me. In the same way that God challenged me, I challenge you to answer these questions for yourself, *"What have you not released completely to God?" "What will you release to God right now, at this moment?"* My story may be unique to me, but it is not unique to God. If you can relate to my story and desire to experience the freedom I am experiencing in God, I challenge you to release everything you are and everything you are not to God, instead of picking up vices like drugs, alcohol and/or sex to numb the pain from the hurts in your life. Trust me when I say, *"God is… a burden bearer, and a heavy load sharer…"* (Malcolm Williams & The Great Faith, "My Everything").

Everything I went through was NECESSARY! Necessary for God to pull out of me each release moment, and to show that I am not an exclusive recipient of His grace, but that all of humanity has the same access to God that I have. It is only when we surrender ALL to Him that we learn the value God has placed on us and have the opportunity to accept it to do great exploits for Him. Being conceived, birthed, raised and/or taught like me was not the problem. The problem was with how I thought, interpreted, and/or responded to all the trials, tribulations, issues, situations and/or problems in my life. I cannot blame the leadership, teachers, ministry staff, nor the pastor for anything I may believe I was not taught because God taught me in my everyday life. He gave me direction and instruction in how to raise my children through the various seasons of their lives. The experiences of my teen years built in me the fortitude I needed to never quit or give up. That same fortitude has kept me focused and prayerful because I knew my children's lives were on the line. It even gave me the strength to institute tough love whenever it was necessary. Today, I am blessed to behold the fruit of the sacrifices I made, the love I shared, the endurance I showed, the support I offered, and the faith God built in me in the lives of my adult children and grandchildren as they carry on a legacy of prayer, Godly strength, wisdom, and love wrought through much pain, hurt, disappointment and tears.

As I sit back and think about my journey and the roads I have traveled, I am grateful to God for allowing me to raise my four children, three girls and one boy, who I affectionately call my hearts! Every opportunity in my life that presented the chance to quit, went unanswered. I was determined not to quit! I am a fighter! It did not matter the circumstances or the situation, I was not going down without a fight. It all started with me learning how to fight with my hands to protect myself; to me using my prayers in spiritual warfare. I love my children, and I was determined the shame and pain I suffered in my youth and young adult life would not damage them like it damaged me. I was their fierce protector, that is until I discovered I was literally squeezing the life out of them during their adolescent years. Every time one of their peers and/or other influences challenged my authority in their life, I gave them a choice; either obey or suffer the consequences. I had unintentionally brought that authoritative rule and dictatorship attitude in my home that I experienced in my childhood. In all honesty, it was the only example I had to use as a guide on how to parent.

CHAPTER 6: There Is a Blessing in the Pressing!

Who is in your corner? GOD, His Angels, Holy Spirit, and the WORD, which is JESUS!!!

By the time I was twenty-one years old, I had become a fighter mentally when I did not realize I was. Let me explain, at age fifteen, I almost killed myself after the rejection and humiliation that occurred on a day, I will never forget during that church service. It is forever cemented in my memory. I could only think about the looks, stares, and hearing the whispers from the church folk all around me. I wanted to cry, but the shock of it all had stunned me into silence. While sitting on that Church bench, I went inward and literally felt my heart break. I asked God to help me, as I stared straight ahead, not wanting to make eye contact with anyone until the service was over and I could get somewhere safe. I was so embarrassed I could not move, but I knew I had to. My maternal grandmother called me over to her, and as I walked over to her with my head down, I could feel the people staring at me. My mind, heart and spirit were crushed. I did my best to focus on the life I was carrying and convince myself not to hurt this child. With all the strength I could muster, I made those last few steps into my grandmother's arms and her embrace. Her hug was a lifeline to me because I felt alone, out of place, and judged. I wished I could disappear where no one could see me.

As usual, outside the Church, the members gathered in groups to talk before leaving the Church property. When I walked out of the Church, the whispers began, the disapproving looks started, and the ostracizing commenced. After what happened during service, how was I supposed to live or even return to this place of hurt, shame and pain? All my life, Church had been a safe place where I was taught about love, faith and prayer during Sunday School, Mid-week Bible study and prayer service, Sunday services, Afternoon Services, VBS, Easter Plays, Christmas plays, etc. I knew about singing in the choir, ushering, memorizing scriptures, and I knew what was expected of me in church, at home and/or in school, but I did not know about life, relationships, and/or who I was, which left an open door for the enemy of my soul to come in like a flood.

The enemy used my emotions, feelings, moments of self-doubt, and newly experienced rejection to create the perfect storm of self-hatred that caused me to fight to get approval at any cost and by any means necessary. I fought mentally, emotionally, and physically. I found myself pleasing people I knew did not like me and seeking acceptance from people who I had used my limited resources to buy their friendship. I hoped they would accept me and fill the void in my life. I just needed someone to love me, to say they loved me, so I could learn how to love myself. I knew I was a disappointment to my mother, our household, and the Church. I knew some people had labeled me as loose and declared I would have several children, be on welfare and not make anything of my life. I was not supposed to hear those conversations, but they spoke loud enough that I could not help but overhear what they were saying. Everything they said hit its bullseye and began its assignment to tear me down one word at a time. It was exactly what the enemy wanted for me. He was out for blood, not just any blood, but my blood.

As a defense mechanism, I learned how to hide in plain sight. What do I mean? I would do everything I was told! I went every place I was supposed to go and presented the mask that all was right in my world/life. Yet, on the inside, I was broken, struggling not to show my hurt nor the tears my heart cried daily. I was shunned and isolated from my cousins, who were my age or close to my age, because I was considered an evil influence. I was treated as if my existence implanted the ideal in their heads to have sex before being married. There was one place where I was not isolated, Church. On Sundays, my cousins and I would meet at Church for a few hours to learn about God, sing, hear a sermon, collect tithes and offering, pray and go home. That was our routine every Sunday.

I was so lonely and deprived of the love and acceptance every teenager needs during their teenage years. After leaving Church, I would ask myself if anyone saw me during the drive home. There did not appear to be anyone who cared or noticed if I was there or not? If they noticed me, why did they not speak or interact with me? Am I that bad? During this time, few people talked to me. I sunk deeper and deeper into despair, and my self-esteem was at an all-time low from my inner turmoil. I would literally cry myself to sleep or sing gospel songs while asking God to help me. I struggled to keep living, but internally a little piece of me died daily.

It is now Thanksgiving Day in 1986, and I am six months pregnant. My aunt, who lived out of town, came to visit me. When she hugged me and told me she loved me, it was as if her words gave me the permission I needed to keep living. I could barely look at her because I felt so ashamed. My heart and mind could not receive the kind words she spoke to me. Even though I was so thankful to hear them. I remember her telling me, *"You're going to have a beautiful baby, and you're going to finish high school and continue your life."* Now my mother had said similar words when we found out I was pregnant, and it comforted me, but when my aunt said it, I believed her. The six months of mentally downing myself and encountering other people's mean words left me feeling lower than an ant. At one of the lowest points in my life, my aunt's words breathed life into me. I glanced at my belly and said, *"I am going to live for this child."* I fought to find my worth, and it was a constant battle. At exactly the right time, God sent my aunt, the church mothers I cherish to this day, and classmates who were my friends to protect and help me through this trying time.

I keep living and learning, and finally I reach my senior year of high school. I had no social life, no boyfriends, and few friends because I do not know how to behave, right? Well, during my senior year, I was focused on graduating. I was not looking to entertain any date requests for prom or anything else. There was one young man who started asking me to the prom. I cannot remember how many times I turned him down. I could not believe anyone was attracted to me. Then out of nowhere, Kendall Priestly, my high school sweetheart found the courage to pass me a note in gym class. When I received it, I was surprised and almost treated it like all the other notes I had received, but I did not. I thought he was handsome, and I accepted his invitation to the prom. I found out a few weeks later that he was a freshman. Now remember, I am a senior. Once it got around, I was going to the prom with a freshman, the males who were seniors got upset. They were offended, I chose a freshman over them. At the root, I believe I chose him because he had the courage to ask me. The fact that I am a senior did not intimidate him. He genuinely liked me, and I am sure his friends thought it was a big deal having a girlfriend who is a senior.

When you thought you were experiencing love, and it was lust, it made me close myself off to anyone who wanted a relationship with me. I was not open to anyone, but I considered "KLP" because he asked me in the simplest and most direct way. Whether he knew I had a child was unimportant. What was important was the fact that he asked me to go with him to the prom. Once again, I turned inward and asked myself what boy was not consumed with having sex or thinking they could easily have sex with me because I already had a child. The innocence of the ask turned my heart from being hard and guarded to considering that someone might actually like me for me. I may not have known who I was back then, but I knew what I would and would not do in my life.

The moments in a person's life are countless, remarkable, and ever-changing. The Almighty God showed me how to turn my struggles into an opportunity to grow. Every time I chose to learn, I grew in spite of the moment designed to hurt me and not help me. I learned alone, which prepared me to help others through and/or overcome similar experiences. God took what hurt me and turned it into a catalyst that propelled me into my God-ordained purpose and destiny. I did not become an overcomer by memorizing scriptures, but because God taught me it does not matter who rejected me, because He loves and accepts me.

The pattern of praying, reading my Bible, and listening to sermons became the strategies I used to live a victorious life for years. It positioned me to see the fruit of the Spirit in my life as part of my testimony. Any love, compassion, wisdom, joy, peace, and/or self-control I had was only because I chose to trust God's will for my life. The moments of release I experienced with God are times when I understood I was the issue in my life. They were also representative of the times when I clearly identified the destructive patterns I had allowed into my life. God is the only One who could free me from thoroughly identifying who I was angry with and why? Would I surrender it to be healed or keep it, and die spiritually? Every time I released the issues, attitudes, and stinking thinking in my heart and mind, I could release those moments and so much more. Since there were so many, I can only share with you the ones God used to mold me into the woman He has called, appointed, and anointed me to be today.

CONCLUSION

The final stage for a butterfly is to become an adult, and for a butterfly they seek to mate so that the process continues as God has in place for it to continue to be a beautiful butterfly. As for me, my transformation spiritually and mentally in the cocoon process and experiences of my life give me the opportunity to appreciate the greatness of God, keeping me even more. Now from ages 36-50, I have become an adult for purpose-oriented assignments in my life. My children grew up and completed high school. My oldest daughter had my oldest granddaughter as a teen, and she recently celebrated her graduation from high school and is preparing for college. All my daughters have been married, and they have blessed me with grandchildren, son-in laws and too many blessings to name.

"Release Moments" gives a glimpse of moments that everyone has in their lives. Even though we do not have the same experiences, we can relate. I care enough about the lives I could touch from my obedience to write this book. Whether people have items they want to release or if they are releasing alcohol, tobacco, and/or prescription or illegal drugs is not important. What is important is that they have begun the process to seek the relief they want and need. Yet when I learned that after I tried to make alcohol my release, God took the desire to drink away from me so that I could learn of Him. He filled me spiritually to only release to Him to get

the true and lasting satisfaction that only He can bring. I now know that you can, because I have been released from anger, doubt, fear, unforgiveness, hopelessness, the spirit of rejection, the spirit of suicide and now live an empowered life. I know that even when things look their worst, I got God! He always gives me a praise, and that gets me through. I have plenty of scars mentally, emotionally, and physically because I allowed God to heal me. The scars show I am alive, and the Holy Spirit allows me to live consistently for Jesus.

There is a cohesive thread of grace that runs through the lives of all believers. However, you cannot truly value the grace assigned to you until you better understand how much is given each moment of the day. Here is what I know about my life. In the same way, Paul was told God's grace was sufficient for him; the grace God has given me has been sufficient in every area of my life as well. In the *"Release Moments"* story, you can clearly see grace in action through my testimony in how my life has brought God glory, and in how the enemy told me lies designed to destroy me. The courage I display with each word written on the pages of this book is reminiscent of the courage God instilled in me to begin the process that has changed, evolved and jump started my life through the moments and experiences I have released to God. It speaks to the fact that every Christian must trust God and be obedient to His word, will and way for their life. A moment of transparency: I would not have written about any part of my life if I was not instructed by God to do so. I did not think the moments in my life had any value, nor did I believe it had the power to impact and/or affect anyone else's life. As God said to me, I also say to you, *"STOP devaluing who I made you to be!"*

It hit me like a ton of bricks! I was devaluing who God made and purposed me to be!!! It started with me having difficulty accepting and/or believing the comment someone made about me when they said, "...*wow, you are so wise!*" I thought to myself '...am I?' If they knew me and the things I have experienced in life, they would not think I am wise. It was then that God impressed upon me to tell my testimony. His words and instructions sparked a level of fear in me, like I have never experienced before. I was scared, but I agreed to do as God asked. Well, maybe not right away. I ran for a few months. When I started this journey to tell of the devastating and life-changing moments that have occurred in my life, I was forty-seven. I am fifty now and I have had seven cycles of seven years and now I am in my Jubilee year. I am grateful for God's grace, allowing me to witness this moment in time. I pray as you read about the moments in my life, you will understand each of us is imperfectly perfect, and we all have been created on purpose and for a purpose. A God-ordained purpose! As you accept the fact that God does not require us to be perfect, He empowers us to surrender our ALL to Him. As we do so, He perfects us because He knows we are unable to make ourselves perfect, which forces us to consider and understand that how a person begins their life and lives their life does not dictate how their life will end.

God empowers us to change the ending of our story daily by changing the choices and/or decisions we make. The greatest and most powerful change agent is Jesus Christ, and without Him there is no hope. But with Him, we learn He is our living hope. As you have read about the difficulties I experienced while releasing pivotal moments in my life, I pray you have recognized the cohesive thread of God's grace running through the threads that make up the fabric of my life and the life of all believers. Like most believers, there have been times when I did not value the grace God has bestowed upon me and it's purposes in my life. I better understand the grace I received from God and how to use it in my daily life. It is my prayer that this book will encourage, enrich, and uplift you to release every moment to God, and take your journey of release moments.

"In His days, Judah will be saved, And Israel will dwell safely; Now this is His name by which He will be called: THE LORD OUR RIGHTEOUSNESS." (Jeremiah 23:6) The person you see now is not who I have always been. You see me after much processing. I have now realized God has given me the wherewithal and fortitude to help others in moments of despair and hurt because of how God healed and delivered me with love and compassion when I went through my season of judgment and cruelty at the hands of others. God was taking me through the emotions, the pain, unforgiveness, and disappointment to teach me how to be a living testimony of what it looks like to go through God's process of change and transformation. I learned how to trust God, share my confidences with Him, and praise Him for bringing me through the moments when I needed to release the trauma, hurt, pain, disillusionment, shame, guilt and unforgiveness to heal me emotionally, mentally, and spiritually, while bringing my mind, body, and spirit into alignment with Him.

When the enemy took me to places and events associated with the hurt, pain and shame designed to keep me in bondage, I resisted. I resisted because I did not want to feel that hurt, pain, guilt, and shame again. What I discovered is that the emotions God required me to experience again were my training ground. It was literally training my heart, mind, spirit, hands, and fingers to be those of a warrior. He knew that as my story poured out of me, I would honor Him in telling the truth that these events, situations and/or trauma happened in my life. I was assigned to tell my story, not to expose others for their treatment or mistreatment of me, but to tell how God strengthened me, encouraged me, and gave me understanding of both His word and His will for my life, which shifted my heart, mind, and spirit from despair to declaration. A declaration to the world that Jesus lives, and He heals. He will take anyone who trusts in Him from the depths of despair to the heights of love, acceptance and approval that only comes from Heaven. Many times, I heard sermons preached about the word of God, but there were no instructions on how to rightly divide the Word of Truth to experience righteous living. God has shown me how to live righteously, because it is His will that I do His will. *"For it is God who works in you both to will and to do for His good pleasure."* (Philippians 2:13) There were many solitary nights of crying, praying, crying some more, praying some more, and then trusting, which led to obeying to get to the Rosetta who boldly and purposefully has written this book. During the process of writing this book, I asked God to make it easier, and I remember Him telling me His grace is sufficient. "And He said to me, *"My grace is sufficient for you, for My strength is made perfect in weakness." Therefore, most gladly I will rather boast in my infirmities, that the power of Christ may rest upon me. Therefore, I take pleasure in infirmities, in reproaches, in needs, in persecutions, in distresses, for Christ's sake. For when I am weak, then I am strong."* (2 Corinthians 12:9-10).

God made me turn away from my need for people to accept and/or approve of me, and completely turn to Him. As God began to strip me of everything that did not measure up to who He says I am, I existed in a lonely place while challenged to build a more intimate relationship with Him. God knows I am a learner and I went about making things make sense to me in a way I could understand. In the same vein, whenever God sends people my way, I meet them where they are and help direct them to where God has determined for them to be. Which is exactly how my God-lessons led to my release moments. Every time I had a release moment from spiritual, mental and/or emotional bondage, my relationship with God grew stronger. It has taught me the importance of lifting my eyes, heart, and spirit to recognize how God replaces what He removes with more of Him. It gives me a better vantage point to behold God, not the nouns (people, places and things) who have negatively affected my life.

There were times when I prayed for God to remove some tough to love and/or unlovable people from my life. God quickly chastised and corrected me, while reminding me that humanity is unlovable because of sin. However, the perfect work He did at Calvary made those who believe in Him part of the Beloved. Romans 5:6-11 AMP explains it this way, *"While we were still helpless [powerless to provide for our salvation], at the right time Christ died* [as a substitute] *for the ungodly. Now it is an extraordinary thing for one to willingly give his life even for an upright man, though perhaps for a good man* [one who is noble and selfless and worthy] *someone might even dare to die. But God clearly shows and proves His own love for us, because while we were still sinners, Christ died for us. Therefore, since we have now been justified* [declared free of the guilt of sin] *by His blood,* [how much more certain is it that] *we will be saved from the* [a]*wrath of God through Him. For if while we were enemies we were reconciled to God through the death of His Son, it is much more certain, having been reconciled, that we will be saved* [from the consequences of sin] *by His life [that is, we will be saved because Christ lives today]. Not only that, but we also rejoice in God* [rejoicing in His love and perfection] *through our Lord Jesus Christ, through whom we have now received and enjoy our reconciliation* [with God]."

I am amazed at how He loves me and how His all-encompassing love has kept me from getting self-righteous and prideful! During those times when I would have thought more highly of myself than I should, God reminded me of the many blessings He has bestowed upon me and my loved ones, and all He has done for me. Yeah, He stepped on my toes, OUCH!!!! He got me straight and kept me straight. He lovingly showed me I was not any better than anyone else, because He processed me the way He did for His glory, and not for me to get the big head. He also assured me that I am not less than anyone. Our only differences are in how He processed each person to produce His glory in their life. God orchestrated a sanctifying process in my life to produce the oil He prepares as the anointing on my life to come forth. It is amazing how the oil He presses out of me daily is also what He uses to sanctify me and keep me in His will. John 17:17-19 NKJV, "*Sanctify them by Your truth. Your word is truth. As You sent Me into the world, I also have sent them into the world. And for their sakes I sanctify Myself, that they also may be sanctified by the truth.*"

One day, I was praying to God about the struggles I experienced while raising my children and for my granddaughter. My heart was breaking, and the stress, strain, and pain I experienced right then came out as tears. It was as if the tears would not stop, and I began to think, '*this is so hard.*' I mentioned earlier about my daughter blaming me for Kendall's death, and sometimes her grief would display itself as anger, and I would find myself fighting her physically and for her in the spirit. During that pity party, God said something to me that immediately caused me to shut up, stop crying, and that snatched me back into reality. He quietly yet succinctly spoke into my spirit these words,

"...*you are complaining about having four children; I have billions of children.*" The loving way He spoke those words caused me to change my complaint into a praise that expressed my thankfulness for God blessing me with my four children. At that moment, I felt strengthened and equipped to raise them through their teenage years, and through the ups and downs that life would throw at us. I had to go through that process, and I am forever grateful that I did. It gave me a new outlook on life and increased my testimony. Now, I can speak to raising my four children by the grace and wisdom of God, and that is why we are all here today.

God took me through a season where He showed me my patterns of behavior and my triggers. It helped me understand why I reacted negatively sometimes, and the moments associated with the behavior that I needed to release. He took each of those moments and created the model that would house the life lessons I would learn from, and ultimately share with and teach to others. People say luck is when opportunity meets preparation. I guess we were lucky on the day I gave a women's day speech to encourage the women. Let me back up and tell the story.

When I was asked to give the speech, my first reaction was to say no and quickly run away, because by accepting the invitation, I would have to give the speech in front of the very people who had talked about me. Instead of running away and saying no right away, I consulted God. During my prayer time, I asked God what He wanted me to do (because I knew what I wanted to do!) and He told me to do it and that He will give me the words to say. This experience showed me how God will speak to you if you ask and seek Him concerning your life, your concerns and when making decisions. Some people have said God does not talk to people. I disagree because He talks to me!

God gave me the Women's Day speech title, "*What's On Your Plate?*" During my speech, I showed a plate with the words God gave me on it. I shared what God gave me to share, and then I took my seat. After the service was over, I had several people ask me where did my message come from, how did I put it together, and who helped me? My reply remained the same with each question, "*God showed me what to do and gave me what to say.*" It was the truth! I guess I was surprised at their reaction because I assumed everyone has conversations with and gets daily directives from God like I do. What I found out was the opposite. Many people talk about God based on experiences they heard about other people having with God, but nothing they have experienced firsthand. They did not know God for themselves. It does not matter how many times you have heard what God has done for others, seek Him for yourself! Use their testimony as your catalyst and press into Him. Get to know Him for yourself! I have never liked to receive information second-hand; I like to go to the source. That is why I ask so many questions. I refuse to assume that being direct is a bad thing. The best thing about it is that it cuts out the middle-man or middle-woman.

One of the biggest lessons I learned while kicking and screaming all the way is to go through your process and stop trying to take shortcuts, because it only leads to detours and more detours. Stop allowing your pride to distract you. Stop believing you know better than God and begin focusing on what God is saying and doing in your life! Stay on straight street and continue moving towards God! When I look at academia's process to get you to an expected end of graduation, a diploma or degree that serves as a witness that you completed the process; I can see the parallelism of it in my life. God knew I can easily grasp concepts and understand methods I have learned during my schooling and home life, which has provided me with the blueprint and structure I have used myself and when I help others.

During moments when my spiritual, mental, and emotional life was in chaos, God would lead me to His word and give me scriptures that taught, strengthened, and prepared me for kingdom work. The Holy Spirit oftentimes gave me understanding and wisdom when guiding me to apply the scriptures to my everyday life. It made sense for me to grasp God's principles, discover the importance of being obedient to God, and witness how those two things helped me navigate my life journey, while providing me with as an example for my children, church members and co-workers as I continued to walk and live out His Word. This was my beginning to confidently hear God, when He spoke to me; that led to me believing and obeying Him. But the minute I tried to make this method the only way God would communicate with me, He quickly corrected me. I cannot box the Sovereign God into what is a comfortable way for me to be on the receiving end of His communication and interaction with me.

God talks and/or interacts with His children in several different ways, and not just one. When God desires to have an experience with you, He knows what to do and how to do it to get your attention so that you know it is Him speaking to you. God provides opportunity after opportunity for His children to do what He has instructed them to do. Even when we do not move or act when prompted, He offers grace to us to act on what He has asked when the opportunity once again presents itself. He is testing their level of obedience. When God asks or instructs you to do something, do it immediately, because as the word of God says, *"obedience is better than sacrifice…"* and when we do not obey, we invite chastisement into our lives and are definitely sacrificing blessings, opportunities, and a chance to grow closer to God.

In my life, God has had me go through many life experiences before the people around me did. He would deliver and/or heal me and send me out to help them with my experience as my reference point. I have found that other believers are more receptive when they know I can personally relate to their anger, hurt, pain and/or the other emotions they may be experiencing, and not only from head knowledge. They seem to learn and connect to my open-heart and my testimony. That is why I lovingly push and/or encourage others, and they respond because they know I really care. Being able to help others encourages me when I see them break out of their spiritual shell and do what God has called them to do. It also gives me the courage to trust God even more as He stretches me and pushes me beyond the borders of my comfort zone.

The experiences I lived through in 2010 strengthened my resolve when talking to and/or ministering to the people God sends me. I can relate to their stories of discouragement because I know all too well what it feels like to be discouraged when all you want is some encouragement to keep going. There were times when I asked God, "Where is my encouragement?" and His response would be sending me to someone or a group of people who needed encouragement. I would say, "God, that is not the answer I wanted to hear". There have been many times when I would read God's word, and specific scriptures would pop out to help and/or comfort me right then. That was one of the things that prompted me to start texting co-workers and a few family members the scriptures God would show me in His word. I would pray that the scriptures would encourage, enrich, and uplift those God inspired me to send them to. It is now eleven and a half years later, and that aspect of my ministry has grown beyond anything I imagined when I started.

The daily texts I send out I think blesses me more than the recipient, and sometimes I wonder if they received its message as intended. And that is when I remind myself, that is God's business! Sometimes people would respond, and I would be encouraged by the simple fact that someone else was encouraged by my act of obedience. As always, God gets the glory for me being committed to completing the tasks as instructed. I love taking life and/or Biblical principles and making them make sense for easy application in people's lives. It brings out the student-mentor and teacher in me. I often tell people that once I make it make sense to you, it is your responsibility to apply the principle to your life. In the same way that dreams do not work unless the person does; the principle is not effective in the person's life until they do the work. It does not just magically happen once you snap your fingers.

I did not get from conception to 50 years without significant guidance, instruction, and love from mentors, teachers, and/or preachers that brought both correction and direction into my life. I needed all that to be the me that I am today. I have learned that what other people have to say about me is none of my business. I am who I am. Anyone with an issue can like it, love it, or hate it. My focus is to please God. He is the only one who will judge or reward me, so if He is pleased, I am satisfied.

In life, we all have moments when we have to release every area of our lives to God. When we do, the release of the old becomes the testimonial message. It is one that cannot be compared to or explained, but it is easily identifiable and seen. It is my prayer that you will be inspired to experience your own release moments with God and is inspired to share your testimony of how you overcame by the blood of the Lamb and the word of your testimony.

I have never claimed to be perfect, but I am perfectly loved by the same God who showed me my purpose. Trust me when I say I am not so special that He will not do the same thing in your life that He has done in mine. Allow forgiveness to permeate your heart, mind, and spirit as it releases all vestiges of the unforgiveness that once lived there. Exchange your bitterness to becoming a better person and follower of Christ. Release the anger you have allowed to dictate your actions and behaviors, and let love lead you into all truth. As you continue to grow into who God has created and purposed you to be, release the hopelessness and grab hold of the hope that God offers as you live a purpose driven life hid in Christ Jesus.

In conclusion, if I am the one assigned by God to reach, teach, counsel and/or love on your loved one, let the words on the pages of this book reassure you that I will obey GOD and love them like I have been loved, no matter how long it takes to love them to life. Please be assured I will treat them like I would want someone to treat my children and/or grandchildren. I realize I am not an army of one. God has many soldiers on the front line doing the work He spoke into and over their lives before the foundation of the world was ever created. I truly believe if each person reaches one person, then this world would be a happier and more loving place. Every time God allows me to meet someone, I am to share my testimony with, I believe I am having a divine encounter with them, and if we both stay connected to God and listen intently for His instructions, our lives will be the better from it.

In Acts 16, God showed me how Paul and Silas had a release moment. He opened my spiritual eyes to see the comparison between their experience and my life. Paul and Silas were beaten and thrown in prison because local people got upset with them for using their authority to cast out an ungodly spirit. Now, after the incident, they prayed and sung praises to God that they were overheard by the other prisoners. God began to show me how when I struggled, and at my wit's end, I would pray and sing praises unto God, and He heard me. While they prayed and sang, the foundation of the prison was shaken, and immediately the doors were opened, and their chains were loosed. The people who were bound are now free in the same place that once held them as a prisoner. The keeper of the prison was about to kill himself when Paul let him know we are all here. In and through this scripture, God showed me how they related to my life and the release moments that happened while I was still in the situation or state from which I needed deliverance. Many ministers will preach about the midnight hour, and the *suddenly* event, but what about the release?

Earlier in the chapter, God deterred Paul from going to Asia by way of Macedonia to preach, and Paul took his companions and obeyed God. Due to Paul's obedience, he and his companions witnessed people believe on Jesus and accept Him as their Lord and Savior. Now that you have the back story, scripture reported Paul cast out an evil spirit, was beaten and imprisoned, and instead of leaving once their chains were loosed, they ministered to the jail keeper. Their obedience to God's instructions led to the jail keeper and his entire household becoming believers. God showed me that what He released me from is not just for me, but for all those attached to me and those who witnessed what God is doing in my life. God did not take me away from my place of hurt, shame and/or disappointment. He showed up where I was and freed me. His presence forced me to understand and deal with my self-imposed emotional, mental and/or spiritual prisons.

He then gave me the opportunity to tell my testimony, in full view of the place that once had me bound. He freed me in the places, city and state that could have easily been my prison, so that others could appreciate His goodness, grace, mercy, and glory in my life. Several people believed on Jesus after hearing my testimony. After the revelation God gave me regarding Paul's life and ministry, my life is forever changed. I will never look at the story of Paul and Silas the same again. What if you were unexpectedly released, and although you received the blessing, it was not for you. God used you as the example of the tremendous work He can do in their life if they would only let Him. In the same way, God showed up strong for Paul and Silas, He will show up strong on your behalf. God has broken the chains that once held me bound, and now I live a victorious life that has had the opportunity to witness many lives being changed, healed, and delivered, because God orchestrated my release moments and blazed a trail for those who would come behind me.

I was empowered to live and grow stronger in my faith, and to authentically help people when I learned the following: How to apologize to my children. For when I took out my job frustrations, life frustrations on them in my responses to them instead of listening to them. God forced me to consider how I could apologize to strangers, but not the ones I loved!! I had to repent for lashing out at them after an intense workday or disagreement with someone and took my frustration out on them because I thought I could control them, but not the other people.

One time while in prayer, I cried out because my first ministry was my household and family, and if I was not doing that correctly, how could I minister to a congregation or anyone else?

Humbled after the Rumble.

Now, I was obstinate before and even after accepting Jesus. I think God used a firm hand to humble me. My training ground was most evident in my interactions with my children and other family members.

I told my girls early in life about the changes their bodies would go through in life. The menstrual cycle and how to use feminine products so that they knew there was a supply in the house, and how to securely keep with them in school. I did not want them to be fearful or terrified. I let them know I was there to help and not harm them. Since I started at age nine, I just assumed my daughters would too, and they were going to be prepared. I also told them what causes girls to become pregnant. I explained what sex was so that they were informed. However, one of my greatest lessons to date is realizing I cannot control the choices they would make in life. The choices they would make would not be because they did not know about the details of life. The Word of God says we perish for lack of knowledge. And when I understood the weight of those consequences, I had no choice but to teach my children.

Learning from being crushed in that church service, I was determined I would not do that to another person, and that I had compassion for male or female teens from that point on.

My maternal grandmother and another mother of the church saved my life on that day. Here I was, once that service was over, I did not move until the Church was almost clear. While holding back the tears, my grandmother called me over and hugged me. She took me into an embrace and said everything was going to be alright.

I did not know how, nor could I receive her words fully, but I believed her. When another mother of the Church embraced me, the tears fell. I needed their encouragement and physical touches. As I sat in the church that day and heard the whisper and felt the eyes on me like I was an exposed criminal I wished I could just die and leave all this behind because it hurt so deeply that I could not put words together to express it. Realtors often say, "*Location, Location, Location!*" On that day in that local Church, it was the location of a teenager being broken and for God to show he had angels in place to embrace me in my brokenness and let me know that this moment was not the end for me.

I understood that I had been wounded internally. In a place where only God could see, but it affected my whole being mentally, physically, and spiritually, and I tried to hide it. I tried to mask my pain.

From that moment on, I was determined to be an advocate to help teen girls who found themselves in that position with love and compassion, and not crush them. Like me, they are in a fragile state, and the pregnancy is merely a symptom of a larger issue. They may have been molested, abused, traumatized and/or hurt. Although my heart was broken, it was open to help others not feel what I was felt.

I gave birth to my firstborn and attended the same church. Going to college and coming home for breaks, my Church family missed the opportunity to witness me growing and maturing. There was no interaction beyond noticing me in service. They did not know me. What they knew about me seemed to be enough for them.

Side note: that is why I am an introvert. When a person claims to know me but does not spend any time with me nor interact with me, they only glimpse moments in my life. For some, those glimpses are all they needed to make assumptions about me.

I thank God for all my release moments that have given me the opportunity to be released from the shame, guilt, fears, and rejection that had turned to anger, because I did not understand or value the person God created me to be. Which I only understood as I studied, read, and believed His Holy Word. I was strengthened to overcome because I wanted God to change what I knew into what I needed to know about Him and grow me up. It took every experience good, bad, or indifferent to get me to this day. The purpose of this book is to share my truth in a manner that is real and authentic, with the hopes of inspiring a person to release their life to God. If I had this type of transparency when I was younger, maybe my life would have turned out differently. But I do not have to wonder or be concerns with ifs because God took all the pieces of my life to make a wonder tapestry for His glory, and no one or nothing can take that away from me. God allowed what man called a mistake, to be born on purpose and for a purpose.

Please do not devalue the perfectly imperfect person you are, but receive forgiveness through repentance, and be filled with the Holy Spirit to be changed internally and externally. It will open your eyes to see who is connected to you rather than family, friends or co-workers that can be positively impacted by the GOD change in you.

Finally, from ages thirty-six to today, I reached the adult stage in my life process. The adult stage is the final stage for the butterfly, and this is where they have been transformed in the cocoon, struggled to get out of the cocoon and strengthened to fly. Butterflies then seek to mate so that they keep the process of life going for them. I pray you realize the importance of reaching adulthood in a spiritual sense, so that eternity is secured for you, but also so that others can grasp, believe, live and continue to help others become free, empowered and able to affect change in others. No person is an island, we are in this earth together, and every time we live to glorify God, we bring a dark and twisted kingdom down.

We need to believe God, act upon our faith in His word and strengthen those around us. Release moments is evidence that I have had not a perfect life, and I did not do everything right and I still struggle with some things in life. I am so grateful to be transparent and say that, and show I am still growing with each breath and the dawning of each new day. It is an opportunity to help others live. God knows that humanity's greatest need is to have an experience with Jesus Christ. That is why He was sent to be our Savior. Our greatest power is the Holy Spirit, which enables, teaches, and shows us how to live Godly. Remember, as you journey through your life, lessons can be learned in complicated ways, or if you are willing to learn the lesson, in beneficial ways. This alone is what matters. There is a lifting and freedom in God, and this world will never compare to that. Be honest and seek the help you need when you need it. Allow the Holy Spirit to teach you how to live by and for God. He will provide the people to help you. You must be willing to complete your process. "*When I was a child, I spoke as a child, I understood as a child, I thought as a child…*" but when I became a woman, I put away childish things. (My emphasis) 1 Corinthians 13:11 NKJV. This makes so much sense! What I perceived as a child was with a child's understanding and point of reference. However, as God's power transformed me from the inside out, I became the mighty vessel of God equipped to encourage, enrich, uplift and partner with others as they go through their release moments. A priceless blessing that keeps giving me strength each day of my life.

RELEASE MOMENTS

Rosetta Priestly

ABOUT THE AUTHOR

Rosetta Priestly is a believer in Jesus Christ and lives life to share and inspire people with this truth in various ways. As an ordained minister of the gospel for over fifteen years, certified biblical counselor for eight years, and an encourager, Rosetta has had opportunities to bless the lives of her family, community, and people around the nation. She is blessed to be the mother of four (Elizabeth, April, Kendra, and Antonio), grandmother of ten, a daughter, sister, cousin, and friend. In January of 2021, she officially launched her blog, called Nuggets When Life Is Rugged.com. The blog gives Rosetta another method to express biblical and inspiring truths to help in everyday life. She is the CEO of Release Biblical Counseling, where she has helped many to biblically address and handle life issues. Rosetta lives in Indianapolis, Indiana where she continues to serve and love on all those that God allows her to encounter on this journey of life.